Listening for God's Call

LEARNING CHURCH

Listening for God's Call: Discipleship and Ministry

Susan H. Jones

scm press

Published in 2014 by SCM Press
Editorial office
3rd Floor
Invicta House
108-114 Golden Lane
London
EC1Y 0TG

SCM Press is an imprint of Hymns Ancient & Modern Ltd
(a registered charity)
13A Hellesdon Park Road
Norwich NR6 5DR, UK

www.scmpress.co.uk

British Library Cataloguing in Publication data

A catalogue record for this book is available
from the British Library

978 0 334 04412 3

Typeset by Regent Typesetting
Printed and bound by
CPI Group (UK) Ltd, Croydon

Contents

Preface

I have written this book for the new *Learning Church Series*, which is designed to support programmes of education and reflection for discipleship and ministry. It is appropriate that one of the first volumes in the series should concentrate on the fundamental theme of God's call.

My thinking behind this book has been shaped by more than a decade's work, first as Director of the Ministry Course at Bangor and then as the Director of the St Seiriol Centre for Christian Discipleship and Ministry in North Wales.

I thank all who have helped to shape the experiences and ideas underpinning this book: Revd Canon Professor Leslie J. Francis and the Bishops of Bangor (first Bishop Tony Crockett and now Bishop Andy John) who have served as co-chairs of the programme in North Wales, but most of all the many people who have responded to God's call in the Diocese of Bangor to explore a vocation as disciples, lay ministers or ordained ministers within the Learning Church.

Susan H. Jones
Lent 2014

1

Listening for God's Call

The idea of call is at the heart of the Christian gospel. The very first thing that Jesus does in Mark's Gospel, before he begins teaching or healing, is to call two pairs of brothers to follow him, Simon Peter and Andrew, James and John. What is not clear from the gospel account is just why these four were chosen to start things off.

A more important question, however, concerns just what these four men were called from and what precisely they were called to. Sometimes the call of Simon Peter and Andrew is construed as the archetypal call into ministry. In that case only a few of us can feel that we are called to follow in their footsteps. Sometimes that call might at least be widened out enough to embrace the call to lay ministries (in a variety of forms). Yet again, the call of Simon Peter and Andrew might be construed as the archetypal call into *discipleship*. In that case many more of us can feel that we are called to follow in their footsteps.

Mark's Gospel goes on to show how Simon Peter, Andrew, James and John did not remain lonely for long. Jesus calls others to join them. We do not know why Jesus called those first four, but we can see what it was in Mark's Gospel that Jesus called them to. Jesus called them to be with him and to learn from him what life is like when God reigns. Simon Peter and Andrew, James and John learned from being with Jesus in two specific ways: from hearing what Jesus said and from seeing what Jesus did. The call to discipleship is the call to be learners, to become a learning people, to be a Learning Church.

In Mark's Gospel there is then a second call. Jesus calls many to be disciples (that is, to be learners), and some of them he calls to be apostles (that is, to be commissioned and sent in his name to do his kind of things). In the gospel tradition, the call to discipleship and the call to ministry are separate and distinct experiences.

The present series of books is concerned – among other things – with ordinary theology, with listening to the ways in which ordinary people speak of their experiences of God. Within the series this particular book is concerned to listen to how ordinary followers of Jesus speak about their experience of being called: to listen to the ways in which they use the word, the ways in which they handle the concept, and the deeper understandings to which the word and the concept point.

Here we meet a number of ordinary people who speak in a variety of ways about their experiences of being called by Jesus. Some speak about their call to be disciples, their call to be part of the Learning Church, their call to serve Jesus in their daily work, their call to participate in a variety of lay ministries, their call to authorized lay ministries or their call to ordained ministries. Most speak about their call in explicitly theological words, using traditional religious phraseology; others, however, talk of their vocation and ministry in less overt terms.

Listening to their many voices reminds us just how varied and rich the Christian experience of call can be. At the same time, listening to these many voices reminds us of the complexity of the ideas of vocation, discipleship and ministry. To chart a way through this complexity, each of the eight following chapters takes the experiences of a small number of these people and engages their voices in conversation with specific parts of the Christian tradition.

As the chapters unfold, conversations draw on particular ways in which we test our experiences of call and vocation alongside major themes from the Bible, major Christian doctrines and the developing understanding and practices of the Christian Church.

Throughout the book, the purpose of these conversations is two-fold. On the one hand, our commitment to belonging to a Learning Church is a commitment to discover the resources of the Bible, Christian doctrine and Church practice, and to see just how these rich theological resources can illuminate our experience of God and open us up to the revelation of God. There is just enough space in these chapters to whet the appetite and to give signposts to places where more can be discovered.

On the other hand, our commitment to belong to a Learning Church is a commitment to go deeper into our own sense of Christian call and Christian vocation. Each chapter is short, but it is not intended to be read quickly. The chapters are punctuated with opportunities to reflect on experience. If the conversation is really to work, it must become a three-way conversation, engaging not only the characters introduced into the narrative and the theological resources but you as the reader as well.

Like all books, this book is written for the individual reader to read in her or his solitude, sitting at a desk, curled up on a sofa, propped up in bed or (more likely) in a crowded and noisy bus or train on the way to work. The opportunities to reflect on experience are just that – opportunities to close the eyes, to shut out the distractions and to look inside.

While this book is written for the solitary reader to read alone, it may be even more profitable if it is read as part of a local education group. Some of the reflective tasks are suitable for wider discussion in such groups. Our eyes can be opened to the revelation of God by going deep inside ourselves and by listening to our own deep reflection. Yet often we need to be startled, challenged or provoked by somebody else saying something else, something we had not really ever considered saying ourselves but that instantly helps to make sense of what we have been trying to articulate.

So here is a book about listening for God's call: God's call into the growing commitment of discipleship, God's call into the unravelling challenges of ministry and God's call to be the Learning Church.

Enjoy the opportunities and learning that this book offers, follow up the ideas it suggests and allow your sense of call and vocation to mature and grow.

2

God's Call in the Bible

Introduction

This chapter begins by listening to the ways in which ordinary Christian people express their experience of 'call' and then sets this experience in conversation with the rich tradition of call in Scripture. Old Testament models of call draw on the accounts of Abraham, Shiphrah and Puah, Moses, Samuel and David. New Testament models of call draw on the accounts of Simon Peter and Andrew, Mary and Martha and Paul. Attention is given to those passages of Scripture that highlight God's call to each individual. The chapter is designed to help us identify the biblical roots for our own sense of call and vocation.

Introducing Alison and John

Alison and John are discussing their call to follow God. For Alison that call began over 40 years ago when she was a young woman. Alison had been brought up in the Church. She was baptized as a baby and had attended church schools, both primary and secondary. Religion was very much part of her life. In her teenage years the Church's influence dwindled and Alison left the Church. It was not until Alison was in her mid-twenties that she felt a gap in her life and heard the call of God to attend church once again and to follow Christ. There was no dramatic conversion, but a sense of coming home, a feeling that God had been guiding her life, even in the years when she felt abandoned by the institutional Church. This journey of call is still ongoing, as Alison continues to discern God's path for her in the quiet contemplative prayer life that is so much a part of her spiritual journey to God. Alison has come over the years to appreciate worship that is quiet and reflective. She is aware that she likes to be challenged in sermons with the big picture and with deep theological questions. She also likes order and structure in her worship.

John's journey began later in life when he was converted to Christianity as a student at university. John's parents had brought him up to be open to the different religions found in his locality. He had Muslim friends and engaged with them in discussion about God, but was always sceptical. At university, John shared a flat with committed Christians and spent many a night discussing Christianity. It was after one particular discussion that his friends invited him to the local student church. The minister was a young man with a deep personal relationship with Jesus. He encouraged John to be open to the Spirit and to welcome God into his life. After one memorable evening, John's life was transformed as he welcomed Jesus into his life. He was baptized and became an ardent and powerful speaker for Christianity and for the Church at university; and he has continued this zeal into his working life. Now John feels called by God to work among the homeless, which is so much part of his active and engaging spiritual life, evidenced by doing and helping others. John is happiest when worship is engaging and when people sing and pray together. He likes to feel through worship and sermons that all are loved and cared for by God. He is keen to make people feel welcomed and to attend to people's needs. But most of all he likes worship to be flexible and open to the Spirit.

TO DO

Draw a diagram or note down:

- your earliest experiences of God;
- key moments as you have grown in faith;
- where you are now.

In what ways have you felt a sense of being called by God to something, or observed a sense of call in someone else?

The call of Abraham

In Genesis 17.1–7 we hear of God's encounter with Abram. Abram is a very old man, a man without much of a future, a geriatric with few prospects; but God calls Abram as the person he is and, in calling him, gives him a new name, Abraham.

Like our opening stories, Abraham's call is personal and particular to him, and it is ongoing. In those stories we recognize that God's call is always ongoing; what God calls us to is based on where we have come from, and so our history with God is deeply linked to who we are.

The call of God is thus particular to individual people. Like Abraham, we are named and known by God. In the Old Testament, names express a person's character and destiny. In giving Abram the new name of Abraham, God is telling us that Abraham will be the 'father of nations'.

In calling Abraham, God is entering into a covenant with him. In verse 1 God outlines what he expects of Abraham, 'walk before me, and be blameless'. Abraham is to trust in the promise and adopt a God-centred attitude, sharing in God's eternal promises in the world. As part of the covenant, God will give him land and children, for Abraham had neither at the time when God called him. In this call, we hear that it is God who takes the initiative; God comes to Abraham and speaks to him. What is clear is that God is the initiator of the covenant. Abraham's response is to fall on his face before the living God and laugh (verse 3). He laughs, and so does Sarah later when she is told she is to have a child. The laughter may be at the improbability of what God is offering them.

Abraham's vocation can only be fulfilled if he has humility and a willingness to listen. Our opening stories suggest it is no different for us.

TO DO

Abraham's encounter with God is told in Genesis 17, but this is a continuation of a calling begun much earlier.

- Read Genesis 12.1–4.
- What does Abraham have to do to respond to God's call?
- Now read how Abraham responds to God in Genesis 15.2–3. How is his response different?

The call of Shiphrah and Puah

At the beginning of the book of Exodus (Exodus 1.15) we hear about the call of two Hebrew midwives, Shiphrah and Puah. For these women, the call of God is heard within the context of their everyday working lives; not unlike John in our opening story who felt called to work with the homeless.

As midwives, Shiphrah's and Puah's vocation is to work in co-operation with the God who brings new life into being. Their calling, like John's, is to a loving, creative, serving work. When faced with a king intending to kill all the descendants of Jacob, these two women stand by their belief in and their fear of God. They refuse to obey the king and they continue their work. There is no sense that God has intervened directly, but what we see is two women listening to the call of God in their daily lives and responding accordingly.

These women do what they can, with the resources they have and the gifts that God has given them, in the situation in which they find themselves. Although these women are not well-known members of society, leaders or policymakers, they have a profound effect on the future of their people. Their faith is seen in their actions, as a consequence of which Moses is spared at birth.

Alison and John are trying to respond to the call of God in the situations in which they find themselves. They are not well-known members of society, but ordinary people like Shiphrah and Puah.

> ## TO DO
>
> Reread the story from Exodus 1.15–21. In what ways do the actions of Shiprah and Puah connect with God's purpose?
>
> In pursuing their calling, Shiprah and Puah engaged in an act of political disobedience. Can you think of more recent examples in which a person/people may be forced into acts of disobedience in order to be true to their calling, like John in our opening story?

The call of Moses

In Exodus 3 we read about the call of Moses who had been saved by the midwives. The call of Moses is once again personal and particular to him. Moses is called from something to something. He is called from his life as a shepherd to bring freedom to the people of Israel, but once again God's call comes while he is doing his ordinary work.

God calls Moses with all of his past history and experience. His past includes education as an Egyptian and his experience of caring for sheep. He has learned from his father-in-law, Jethro, the priest of Midian, and from his own experience as husband and father. God uses these experiences, as well as Moses' experience as an escaped murderer, to lead the people of Israel to freedom. Moses was a reluctant leader and, as the call of God progresses, he offers more and more objections. But God responds each time, until Moses obeys God's call. For many, including the call of John in our opening story, hearing God's call is no immediate guarantee of following God. Excuses are made and unworthiness is protested, but in the end Moses and others agree.

Moses' call was not in isolation; it is set within the context of other people's call from God, the call for freedom. Pharaoh's daughter was called and played her part; likewise many others heard the call and responded. This call for liberation is still being heard, and John's call to work with the homeless could well be seen as a call from God to liberate the poor.

TO DO

Moses was called to liberate his people from oppression. Reflecting on this call, can you think of others who have been called to liberate people from oppression? Were any of them reluctant leaders?

The call of Samuel

In 1 Samuel 3, we read about the call of the boy Samuel. Samuel, we are told, was ministering to the Lord under Eli. It is not Samuel who recognizes the call of God, but Eli. The scene is set at night. Eli, old and with poor eyesight, is in his room. The young Samuel is lying in the sanctuary where the ark of Yahweh was resting. Despite the 'quaintness' of this story, it is actually concerned with political power. The writer gives us clues as to the direction the narrative will take. Although Eli cannot see well, he will eventually 'see' who is calling Samuel and point to Yahweh's part in it.

Eli is a model of ministry. Even though we know his family is condemned, and Eli himself seems powerless to do anything, he is wise enough in the faith to direct the young Samuel to the point where he can 'hear' what Yahweh has to say to him.

Moreover, Eli has the courage to hear that word from the lad, even though it is critical of his own interests. He is a model of self-effacement, as he seeks to discern the way of the Lord in his troubled world. In a politically charged and uncertain society, it is in the innocence of a young lad, the wisdom of an old man willing to yield his part in affairs, and the joyous song of a young mother (1 Samuel 2.1–10) that we hear of the way of the Lord and God's call upon these people.

In our opening story, it was the friends of John who heard the call of God for him. It was his fellow housemates who took the time to answer John's questions of faith, to guide him towards God and to help him respond to God's call.

TO DO

Reflecting on the call of Samuel, can you think of a modern-day example in which someone is called by God and someone else interpreted that call?

The call of David

In 1 Samuel 16, we read about the calling and anointing of David. God's choice of David was a personal call. The prophet Samuel called all the other sons of Jesse, who were apparently more appropriate candidates for king, but God specifically wanted David. God chose the youngest, the one not considered important enough to be present. God called the 'unconventional David', the one his father Jesse least expected to be the model of Israel's Messiah (Spina, 2001).

David, like Alison and John, did not initially discern the purpose of his calling. David's first public step into obeying the call of God resulted in the defeat of Goliath. It was accomplished by a faith nurtured in secret and through skills gained over the years. In time he became the greatest king of Israel, one whom the prophets saw as an icon for the Messiah. His story, like the stories of Alison and John, will be part of a much bigger story. The story of faith goes far beyond a small and often narrow understanding of God's call. David's story, like the story of Alison and John, is a story of journeying: in David's case from shepherd boy to sovereign king, with many twists and turns and with remarkable skills developed on the way. The same is true for Alison and John.

TO DO

David was called by God and anointed to be king, but David's journey of faith did not end there. In 2 Samuel 7.1–17 we hear that God said 'No' to David.

- Why do you think God said 'No' to David?
- What resulted from this no?
- On what sort of journey did God's call take David, and how does David's call reflect our own sense of call?

The call of Simon Peter and Andrew

The call of Simon Peter and Andrew is found in the Synoptic Gospels (Matthew 4.18–19; Mark 1.16–18; Luke 5.9–10). The Gospels of Matthew and Mark have almost identical stories. The call of the two brothers happens while they are going about their everyday work of fishing; they are casting nets into the sea when Jesus says to them, 'Follow me and I will make you fish for people.'

Like the call of Elijah in 1 Kings 19.19–21 and the call of the Old Testament prophets in general where God calls people from their everyday existence (e.g. Amos 7.15), Jesus expresses the divine initiative in calling people to discipleship.

In the time of Jesus, rabbis did not seek out students, but students sought out rabbis. In the story of the calling of Simon Peter and Andrew, as is true in the calling of Alison and John, it is Jesus who takes the initiative. Jesus goes to Simon Peter and Andrew; they do not come to him. He sees them; they do not see him. He speaks to them; they do not speak to him.

The big question down the centuries has been: 'How do people become disciples of Jesus Christ?' Alison and John came to be disciples of Christ in very different ways, but what is clear is that, when the call is heard, people follow.

The story of the call of Simon Peter and Andrew in Matthew's Gospel is trying to answer the question of call. The writer of Matthew answers the question by showing Jesus standing disruptively in our midst and calling us not to admire him or accept his principles, not even to accept him as our personal saviour, but *to follow him.*

A reasonable response to Jesus' command, 'Follow me', would be, 'Where are you going?' The fishermen, like Alison and John, do not know the destination; they must learn it along the way.

Like Alison and John, people become disciples of Christ in different ways: some through dramatic suddenness and some through a slow and painful struggle; others cannot point to a specific call at all, because having been born and bred in the faith they cannot remember a time when they were not believers. For the writer of Matthew's Gospel, there is one common denominator. People become disciples by the power of Jesus' word; they follow because Jesus has spoken to them, and his word generates faith (Boring, 1994).

TO DO

Reflecting on your own call to discipleship, do you think that you have a sense of hearing a call? If so, write down how the 'call to follow' came about for you, and how it has impacted on your own life and those around you.

If you have not experienced anything like this, is it proper to interpret the circumstances and story of your life as a form of 'call'?

The call of Mary and Martha

The story of Mary and Martha (Luke 10.38–42) is the story of two sisters called by God to follow Christ in two very different ways (Francis and Atkins, 2000). Like Alison and John, they are two very different people. Martha is like John in our story; both could be seen as archetypal extroverts. Martha is excited by the arrival of visitors. John is excited to talk about his faith with others. Both enjoy and are occupied with all the social interaction. Martha engages with her visitors and draws energy from them.

Mary, like Alison, is the archetypal introvert. Mary quietly withdraws into herself when the visitors arrive and gets exhausted by the social interaction. What Mary and Alison do is sit at the visitors' feet and become centres of stillness and quiet.

Martha, like John, is called by God as a person who takes notice of the practicalities of hospitality. She prepares the food and caters for the needs of people. On the other hand, Mary, like Alison, is called by God to listen to Jesus. She engages with his vision and asks wide-ranging and wide-reaching questions. Mary looks at the ideas of Jesus and uses her own imagination to see the big picture.

Martha, like John, is called by God to use her concern for the well-being of her guests and to engage with matters of the heart. She is concerned with the feelings of her guests and is keen to make them feel welcome. Mary, like Alison, is called by God to be concerned with matters of the head. She sets her priorities and welcomes the challenge of Jesus' teaching.

Martha, like Alison, is called by God to be the well-organized person, disciplined in her outside world. She needs to plan the supper, and she needs order and routine in her life. Mary, like John, is called by God to be open and flexible. She lets supper take second place so she can listen to Jesus' conversation. Mary and John like their outside world to be flexible and spontaneous.

Both Mary and Martha, like John and Alison, are called to serve Jesus, but in very different ways.

TO DO

Mary and Martha have very different personalities. How well do you think the Church responds to the call of such different people?

In your experience, have you seen evidence of the Church being inclusive of all personality types?

Who do you think the Church values more, Mary or Martha?

The call of Paul

Paul's conversion on the road to Damascus (Acts 9.1–19; 22.3–21; 26.4–23) is often quoted as an example of a sudden dramatic conversion to a faith in Jesus. John in our story had such a conversion, but the conversion of both characters comes from a history of exploring faith. For Paul, what occurred on the Damascus road was a climactic event, a literal conversion in the sense that he was going one way and now found himself going in a different direction (Coggan, 1998). He had been turned around. It was as if he had been running from God, then turned round and found himself face to face with God, who had been calling him with infinite compassion. Somehow, the person of Jesus was central to this change. As Paul was later to write: 'the light which is knowledge of the glory of God' was 'in the face of Jesus Christ' (2 Corinthians 4.6).

The journey that Paul travelled was a conversion from one sect of first-century Judaism to another; that is, conversion from a mainline sect (Pharisee), which wished to reinforce Israel's separation from the Gentile world, to a sect that understood Israel's commission as 'a light to the nations' to include the Gentiles.

Like Alison and John, Paul's conversion happens within a faith community that confirms Paul's salvation and safeguards his prophetic vocation. This community is there to support the new disciple, emphasizing the fact that discipleship is far too demanding for the individual alone (Wall, 2002).

Like Alison, Paul had found peace. He could look into the face of Christ and know that all was well. He did not have to abandon the faith of Judaism; there was continuity with the old faith. What is clear, however, is that Paul began a new journey. That new journey made Paul not only an 'apostle for the Gentiles' (Romans 11.13), but a founder of Christian communities, an interpreter of the Christ-event and the first Christian theologian whose interpretation we have inherited (Fitzmyer, 1993).

Like John, Paul could not keep the revelation of Jesus Christ to himself; he had to tell the good news of Jesus Christ to everyone.

TO DO

Reread all three of the conversion stories of Paul in Acts (Acts 9.1–19; 22.3–21; 26.4–23).

- What are the similarities and the differences?
- Why do you think the differences are there?

Conclusion

This chapter has explored the idea of call in Scripture. It has looked at Old Testament models of call and drawn on the accounts of Abraham, Shiphrah and Puah, Moses, Samuel and David. It has looked at New Testament models of call and drawn on the accounts of Simon Peter and Andrew, Mary and Martha and Paul.

In the Hebrew Scriptures we hear that God calls people into relationship, makes a covenant with them and reminds them to keep that covenant. We hear of people called from within their everyday lives to follow God. They are ordinary people trying to live and work according to the purpose of God. We hear also God calling the whole community, but how far the community responds depends on whether individuals hear and respond, and encourage others to hear and to respond (Chapman, 2004).

In the New Testament we hear that Jesus calls people. We hear about ordinary fishermen called to leave their nets and to follow. We hear of two women called in different ways to respond to and serve Jesus, as the people whom God made them to be. We hear of conversion and the role of the community in enabling disciples to follow Christ.

The call in Scripture helps us recognize that God calls us from different places, as different people with different skills and gifts. God also calls us with our own particular personal histories, limitations and failings. Our calling is unique and special, and like all Christian discipleship it finds its roots and identity in Jesus. As disciples, as people called by Jesus, we are expected to model our lives on Jesus. In other words, disciples are called to be imitators of Christ (Stephenson, 2004).

Further reading

Boring, M. E., 1994, *The Gospel of Matthew* (The New Interpreters Bible), Nashville, TN: Abingdon Press.

Chapman, I. A., 2004, 'The Call of a People', in C. Richardson (ed.), *This is our Calling*, pp. 13–21, London: SPCK.

Coggan, D., 1998, *Meet Paul: An Encounter with the Apostle*, London: Triangle.

Fitzmyer, I. A., 1993, *According to Paul: Studies in the Theology of Paul*, New York: Paulist Press.

Francis, L. J. and Atkins, P., 2000, *Exploring Luke's Gospel*, London: Mowbray.

Spina, F. A., 2001, 'Fourth Sunday in Lent Year A', in R. E. van Harn (ed.), *The Lectionary Commentary: Theological Exegesis for Sunday's Texts*, pp. 182–5, London: Continuum.

Stephenson, D., 2004, 'The Call of Disciples', in C. Richardson (ed.), *This is our Calling*, pp. 55–66, London: SPCK.

Wall, R. W., 2002, *The Acts of the Apostles* (The New Interpreters Bible), Nashville, TN: Abingdon Press.

3

Discipleship in Today's Church

Introduction

This chapter begins by listening to what discipleship means for a variety of ordinary Christian people: to the parents who have just had their infant baptized as a disciple, to the teenage boy and to the long-serving church member. These accounts are then set in conversation with contemporary theologies of discipleship across various church traditions. The chapter is designed to help us identify our own sense of call and vocation to discipleship.

Introducing Jessica, Stephen, Aled and Alice

Jessica and Stephen have just had their baby, Sophie, baptized in their local church. They have been attending church as a family for the past six months in preparation for the baptism. Jessica had been brought up in the Church, but had lapsed since going to university and beginning work. Stephen has not as yet been baptized, but has felt drawn to the Church by his daughter's baptism. Although Stephen is yet to commit to Christ through the rite of baptism, he is active in the local church as part of the men's group. Jessica has reconnected with the Church through her daughter's baptism and is beginning to explore what it means to be a disciple of Christ. As a family, they feel as if they are on a journey, a journey that is leading them towards a deeper faith in Christ.

Aled is 14 years old and attends church with his grandmother. He has regularly attended church with his grandmother since the age of three. Aled was baptized as a baby and has recently received communion for the first time. Before receiving communion Aled began a process of preparation, which is still ongoing. Aled now assists in the church as an altar server and attends the youth club that meets at the church. Aled, like some other young people in the youth group, feels that God is part of his life, but struggles with the many different competing claims of activities in the community, like football, rugby and computer games.

Alice is in her sixties and has attended the local church since she was married in the 1970s. Alice's journey of discipleship began when she wanted to be married in church and, in preparation for her marriage, got baptized and confirmed. In the years following her baptism, Alice began her discipleship journey and became dedicated to helping others. Alice has been a long-standing member of the Mothers' Union and has worked as their information-sharing secretary. Since retiring, Alice has been part of a university-accredited course run in partnership with her church and has been studying more about her faith. This study has given her confidence to live out her discipleship through working as a lay chaplain at her local cathedral and through work as an administrator at the cathedral foodbank. Alice is quite clear that she is called to discipleship, but not to authorized ministry within the Church.

Discipleship in the Bible

The previous chapter explored the idea of God's call through different characters in the Bible. This chapter looks at the call to Christian discipleship. The term 'disciple' occurs many times in the New Testament, but only in the Gospels and Acts. It is used as a description for the Twelve who, according to the gospel, originally followed Jesus, and also as a description for a wide range of Jesus' followers. To be a disciple is to be a follower of Christ. Discipleship in the Bible is characterized by establishing a relationship with Jesus and not merely attending to his teaching. Dunn (1992), in his book *Jesus' Call to Discipleship*, suggests that the call to discipleship in the early Church was the call to faith in the risen Christ, rather than simply repeating the message of Jesus. He goes on to say that the characteristics of discipleship are those seen in the life and work of Jesus.

It is in the Gospel of Matthew that the Great Commission informs the disciples of Jesus that Christians are not just called to be disciples, but are also called to make disciples of others.

> Now the eleven disciples went to Galilee, to the mountain to which Jesus had directed them. When they saw him, they worshipped him; but some doubted. And Jesus came and said to them, 'All authority in heaven and on earth has been given to me. Go therefore and make disciples of all nations, baptizing them in the name of the Father and of the Son and of the Holy Spirit, and teaching them to obey everything that I have commanded you. And remember, I am with you always, to the end of the age.' (Matthew 28.16–20)

This is the task of Christians today, to 'make disciples' of all people. In making disciples the Church is called not just to fill the churches, but to create environments where people grow and develop in their faith, so becoming mature, long-term followers of Christ.

TO DO

When thinking of your own journey of faith:

- Do you remember when you became a disciple of Christ?
- Was it a dramatic conversion that began a process, or was it a process that began when you were very young?
- Who has guided you in your discipleship?

The word 'disciple' has been used to describe the Twelve whom Jesus called to be his followers, but it also refers to all who are trying, and who have tried down the ages, to follow the way of Jesus. Based on the Latin word *discipulus*, which means 'pupil' or 'student', the words 'disciple' and 'discipleship' carry the often hidden message that the quest for authentic, positive Christian living involves learning (Astley, 2007; Cherry, 2011). As Alice recognizes in her discipleship the need for learning, she has chosen in her retirement to follow an accredited course. In her early married life, when she began her journey of discipleship, there were very few opportunities for learning the faith and she never experienced a programme of catechesis or even confirmation classes.

Jessica, Stephen, baby Sophie, Aled and Alice have all come to faith and discipleship in different ways. There is no single way to become a disciple of Christ; it can take very many different forms. For some people, like Jessica and Aled, they cannot remember a time when they did not believe; for others, becoming a follower of Christ was through an instantaneous conversion experience.

In the past, some forms of mission have focused on evangelistic events where people have been encouraged to make instant decisions about following Christ. David Watson and Billy Graham promoted evangelistic events that sought this type of conversion. While recognizing that people need to make a decision about following Christ, the emphasis today is often more on discipleship as a journey rather than on a crisis event.

In the early centuries of Christianity, the process of making disciples was through baptism. Baptism, however, was part of a much fuller rite of initiation that included the laying on of hands, anointing and sharing for the first time the eucharistic meal. In other words, Christian initiation was celebrated in a continuous rite involving what are now called the sacraments of baptism, confirmation and Eucharist. Alice's journey of discipleship began when she wanted to be married in church and, in preparation for her marriage, she got baptized and confirmed in one liturgical act at an Easter Eve liturgy in her local church. For Alice, however, there was no instruction or learning. She simply spoke to her local vicar and within weeks was baptized, confirmed and received her first communion.

Catechesis

In the early centuries of Christianity, before receiving the sacrament of baptism, people were prepared through an educational programme known as catechesis. Various models of catechesis were developed in the first four centuries of church history. There was no definitive programme and differences in emphases, content and length can be seen. On average, the whole process from first interest to being baptized, confirmed and receiving communion for the first time lasted around three years (Kelly, 1999). Within the journey there were three clear stages, each one marked by certain symbolic rites.

The first stage was the enquiring stage. The non-believer expressed the wish to know more about Christ, the Church and the Christian life. Such people were called enquirers. They learned about Christ and the Church and, when they showed a clear commitment, they were formally welcomed by the bishop and the community in the rite of entry into the catechumenate.

The second stage was the catechumenate and the candidates were called catechumens. They were acknowledged by the local community and were allowed to call themselves Christians. In the catechumenate, the preparation of the catechumens became more systematic. They took part in Sunday worship, but were dismissed after the homily and before the Eucharist. When they were ready for baptism, they would be formally called by the bishop, in the name of the Church, in the rite of election. The catechumens had now become the elect.

The third stage was called the period of enlightenment. The candidates' period of preparation was intense as Easter approached. The enlightenment reached its climax on Holy Saturday night with the baptism, confirmation and Eucharist. The candidates became full members of the Church. The journey did not end there, and the new Christians continued their learning from Easter to Pentecost. This was the period of mystagogy and during it the candidates were taught about the 'mysteries' they had undergone.

From the fourth century onwards, this process of catechesis declined as infant baptism became the norm. The Roman Catholic

Church, however, has (since the Second Vatican Council) restored the full process. The catechesis process is an educational programme in the faith of children, young people and adults, which includes the teaching of Christian doctrine. Aled began his catechesis process a few years ago before he received his first communion. This process continues as part of the youth club he attends.

TO DO

Thinking about your own journey of faith:

- Have you grown as a Christian?
- Have you undergone a catechetical programme?
- What do you think would be the positive and negative aspects of running a programme for those enquiring about faith today?

Most churches believe that it is through the rite of baptism that the individual (infant or adult) becomes a member of Christ, by being incorporated into the Church. This is certainly true for Jessica and Stephen; they have had their baby baptized because they wanted Sophie to be a member of the Christian family and a disciple of Christ. Although Jessica has lapsed in her faith over a number of years, she has always believed that she is still a disciple of Christ. The baptism of Sophie has allowed Jessica to reconnect with the Church, rediscover her call to discipleship and share in the ministry of the whole people of God.

Ministry of the whole people of God

Over the past 30 years, the Church has been developing an understanding of the ministry of the whole people of God, founded on and celebrated in baptism. It is now generally accepted that the ministry of the baptized is foundational to the life, witness, mission and ministry of the whole people of God.

Liturgically and theologically, baptism is understood as the sacrament of initiation into the community of faith for a life of service (*diakonia*) and witness. The development of this understanding can be seen in the work of the World Council of Churches and their seminal document *Baptism, Eucharist and Ministry*, which became known as the Lima document (World Council of Churches, 1982). The document is the result of a 50-year process, which began at the Faith and Order Conference of the World Council of Churches meeting in Lausanne in 1927.

In the context of the 'calling of the whole people of God', the document states that 'in a broken world God calls the whole of humanity to become God's people'. It goes on to say:

> The Holy Spirit bestows on the community diverse and complementary gifts. These are for the common good of the whole people and are manifested in acts of service within the community and to the world. They may be gifts of communicating the Gospel in word and deed, gifts of healing, gifts of praying, gifts of teaching and learning, gifts of serving, gifts of guidance and following, gifts of inspiration and vision. All members are called to discover, with the help of the community, the gifts they have received and to use them for the building up of the Church and for the service of the world to which the Church is sent. (World Council of Churches, 1982, p. 20, para. 5)

Alice can relate to this understanding of the calling of the whole people of God. She sees her discipleship in terms of acts of service within the community and the world. Her work with the Mothers' Union brings her into contact with the worldwide Church, and her experience with the foodbank brings her into contact with those in need in the local community. Her study has given her the confidence to recognize that the Holy Spirit has given her many gifts to serve the Church. These gifts, she believes, include the gifts of prayer and service, the gifts of guidance and following, the gifts of love and compassion, and many others.

Jessica and Stephen have become open to the call to discipleship through their daughter's baptism. Jessica and her daughter have responded through baptism to the call to follow Christ: both have begun the journey and received the gift of the Holy Spirit. Stephen, on the other hand, is yet to commit through baptism to a life of service within the Church. He is very much at the beginning of discovering what it means to be a follower of Christ, but has begun to offer help to the church through the men's group, which looks after the church building.

Aled is beginning to discover what it means to be a follower of Christ. He has discovered the role of assisting in the church as an altar server. The many gifts the Holy Spirit given to him at baptism are beginning to be discovered, but Aled's journey into believing for himself is only just starting.

Alison, Jessica, Stephen and Aled belong to churches that have strong lay leadership, which recognize the call of the whole people of God and also the role of the ordained person. One of the problems associated with the Lima document is the lack of consensus among the Churches regarding how the life of the Church is to be ordered. This leads to the question:

> How, according to the will of God under the guidance of the Holy Spirit, is the life of the Church to be understood and ordered, so that the Gospel may be spread and the community built up in love? (World Council of Churches, 1982, p. 20, para. 6)

In asking this question, the Lima report moves away from the ministry of the whole people of God to the ministry of the ordained. This results in the following statement: 'the ministry of those ordained is constitutive for the life and witness of the church' (p. 20, para. 8).

The Lima report then loses its earlier emphasis on the 'diverse and complementary' gifts of the Spirit for the strength, witness and service of the whole community (Pickard, 2009). This move seems to weaken the call for all members to discover the gifts they have received for the building up of the Church and to re-emphasize the call to ordained ministry. Yet many people, like Alice, do not feel called to ordained or even authorized lay ministry, but to discipleship.

Since the publication of *Baptism, Eucharist and Ministry*, there has been growing interest in the Churches about the ministry of the whole people of God. Titles such as *Total Ministry* (Zabriskie, 1995) have given encouragement to develop different lay ministries. In this book, Zabriskie states that all baptized Christians have a vocation. This vocation, he goes on to say, is 'outlined and given direction in the baptismal covenant'. Zabriskie's definition of total ministry is the recognition of the ministry of all the baptized.

On this account, baptism has been seen as the entry into lay ministry, but this leads to a number of problems. First, the term 'ministry' can be used to include ordained ministry, authorized lay ministries, other lay ministries, and many aspects of discipleship common to all Christians – including, for example, prayer and pastoral care.

In the 1970s in particular, 'ministry' became the watchword (Platten, 2010). It came with a variety of qualifiers: auxiliary ministry, collaborative ministry, lay ministry and every-member ministry, often built on the idea of the 'priesthood of all believers'. The question was not 'Do you have a ministry?', but 'To what particular ministry are you called?'

TO DO

What do the terms 'auxiliary ministry', 'collaborative ministry', 'lay ministry' and 'every-member ministry' mean to you?

Which of these terms are used in the church of which you are a member?

In the Church of England, the Tiller Report (1983) embraced the approach of 'every-member ministry' as both a theological and pragmatic response to the perceived crisis in vocations to ordained ministry. What emerged from this approach was an ambiguity as to what ministry is. Helen Oppenheimer wrote of this difficulty as follows:

> The trouble is that ministry, much more than priesthood, is what one might call a greedy concept. The notion of ministry tends to gobble up everything into itself so that it becomes impossible to sort out what is not ministry. All are ministers but some are more ministers than others. (Oppenheimer, 1979, pp. 11–19)

Robert Hannaford also recognizes the problems associated with every-member ministry. He says: 'If "every-member ministry" simply means that every Christian has his or her own ministry, the result is a radically individualistic understanding of the Church itself and not a genuinely expanded theology of ministry' (Hannaford, 1996, p. 23).

The second issue concerns the relationship of ministry to baptism and is implicit in the Lima document. It has become usual to think of baptism as a sacramental sign for a vocation to Christian ministry, in whatever form this may take. The implications of this understanding overlooks the primary significance of baptism as initiation into the community of the Church. The connection between baptism and ministry is through an individual's incorporation into the ministerial community of the Church. Hannaford states: 'Baptism does not so much bestow a ministerial calling as call someone into the ministerial community of the church' (1996, p. 43). He goes on to argue that discipleship, not ministry, is the more inclusive category. The Christian life is a life of discipleship; ministry is an expression of apostleship. In baptism, all Christians are called to be disciples of Christ. Discipleship is intrinsic to being a baptized follower of Jesus Christ. Ministry is something that is subsequently discerned. All ministers should be disciples; but not all disciples are necessarily ministers (Church of England, 2007a, pp. 116–17).

Paul Avis, in his book *A Ministry Shaped by Mission*, also suggests that the 'notion of ministry has become so broad that it is in danger of becoming meaningless' (Avis, 2005, p. 43). He goes on to suggest that 'in some contexts of usage ministry seems to have become equivalent to everything a Christian does in his or her life of discipleship' (p. 44). Avis concludes that 'Christian actions are acknowledged by us to be expressions of ministry if they are recognized, expected or mandated by the Church, if they have a public dimension and if they are subjected to some kind of accountability and oversight' (p. 46).

Education for discipleship

Alice has been quite clear in her understanding of the Christian faith that she is a disciple and is called as a disciple to do acts of service. She does not feel that baptism has led her into ministry but into discipleship. That discipleship involves learning and reflecting on that learning in the light of experience. Disciples are called to transform and be transformed, as the first disciples were in their journey with Christ.

Graham Carter, President of the Methodist Church from 2006 to 2007, called for the Church fully to take up the challenge of discipleship. In his Conference address, Carter commented: 'The kingdom needs wholehearted disciples. Nothing must be allowed to get in the way.' In particular, the new president pointed out that a problem often encountered by the Church was that too often discipleship was equated with holding office. He went on to say that Christ calls all people to serve him with the whole of their lives, and that discipleship is about how you live at work, at home and in the community. Although he accepted that this was a tough challenge, he urged the Church to renew its identity as the body to provide practical support for people's discipleship in a complex world.

The development of support for discipleship training has been part of the Churches' agenda since the publication by the Church of England of the Hind Report, *Formation for Ministry within a Learning Church* (Archbishops' Council, 2003). The idea of education for discipleship was subsequently developed in the document *Shaping the Future: New Patterns for Training for Lay and Ordained* (Archbishops' Council, 2006). Both publications express the desire for the whole Church to become a Learning Church.

Discipleship is understood as the 'whole-life response of Christians to Jesus Christ'. With this understanding, *Shaping the Future* develops an understanding that discipleship is the calling of all Christians and that those who respond to God's call to follow share explicitly in God's mission and ministry in the world. Learning should then connect with life experience and with ministry and mission at the grass roots. A framework for educating disciples is shaped by the context and needs of learners – the needs of learners in the world and not only in the Church.

This has been Alice's experience as she has followed an education for discipleship course. Alice feels that she has been able to reflect on what she has learned through the Bible, the doctrines of the Church and the history of the Church in the context of her local church and community.

TO DO

Looking back on your Christian journey, note down whether you think you are called through baptism to ministry or to discipleship.

What, in your experience, are the differences between discipleship and ministry?

Conclusion

This chapter has explored an understanding of Christian discipleship that is distinct from Christian ministry. The chapter began by investigating discipleship in the Bible. It presented the notion that while people are called to discipleship they are also called to 'make' disciples.

In terms of calling people to discipleship, the chapter explored how the early Church developed a catechetical programme to initiate people into the Church. These programmes were varied and lasted around three years. With the increase in infant baptism, after the conversion of the emperor Constantine in the fourth century, the catechetical programme declined, but the chapter went on to explore how the Roman Catholic Church has reinstated and developed a catechetical programme since the Second Vatican Council.

The second half of the chapter explored the notion of the ministry of the whole people of God or 'every-member ministry'. It looked at the advantages and disadvantages of this understanding and came to the conclusion that all Christians are called to discipleship but that not all are called to ministry.

Finally, the chapter briefly looked at the development of what has become known as education for discipleship and how the Church is moving towards becoming a Learning Church.

Further reading

Adair, J., 2000, *How to Find Your Vocation*, Norwich: Canterbury Press.

Astley, J., 2007, *Christ of the Everyday*, London: SPCK.

Avis, P., 2005, *A Ministry Shaped by Mission*, London: T. & T. Clark.

Cherry, S., 2011, *Barefoot Disciple*, London: Continuum.

Dunn, J., 1992, *Jesus' Call to Discipleship*, Cambridge: Cambridge University Press.

Hall C. and Hannaford R. (eds), 1996, *Order and Ministry*, Leominster: Gracewing.

Kelly, R., 1999, *Exploring the Sacraments*, Buxhall: Kevin Mayhew.

Pickard, S., 2009, *Theological Foundations for Collaborative Ministry*, Farnham: Ashgate.

World Council of Churches, 1982, *Baptism, Eucharist and Ministry* (Faith and Order Paper no. 111), Geneva: World Council of Churches.

Zabriskie, S. C., 1995, *Total Ministry: Reclaiming the Ministry of all God's People*, New York: Alban Institute.

4

Called to Be Lay

Introduction

This chapter begins by listening to how ordinary Christians express their sense of call to their daily vocations: a gardener speaks of her vocation to work in a local park; a teacher speaks of his vocation to teach in a local school; a single mum talks of her vocation to work part-time in a local cafe as she raises her child. These accounts are set in conversation with the Christian tradition that God is concerned with the whole of life and challenges the notion that vocation to discipleship is incomplete without accompanying vocation to a church-based ministry. In this context, God's call is highlighted in respect of a whole range of 'secular' occupations. This chapter is designed to help us assess our own sense of call and vocation within our daily lives.

Introducing Sue, James and Grace

Sue has worked for a number of years with the local council, caring for the parks in the vicinity. Sue left school at 16 and did an apprenticeship at a local National Trust property. Here she learned about plants and how to use different ones to enliven and enrich the environment in which she worked. Sue began her Christian life as a member of the church youth group and has felt called to work with God's creation since a teenager. Sue feels closest to God in the natural environment. She believes firmly in the creator God and that she is called to be a steward of God's creation. Sue gives talks to local organizations about her work; she also talks about how her faith and understanding of God is part of her work.

James is the headteacher at the local Church of England voluntary aided primary school. When James came to the school a few years ago he was a new Christian and felt called to serve God as a headteacher in a church school. In this role James has run the school on Christian values, which he has learned as a Christian disciple. These values include, in particular, kindness, fairness and good self-esteem. James has modelled and worked an ethos into the school where every person counts, from the cleaners to the governors. Teachers, classroom assistants and parents work in teams, with their focus on the best learning environment for the children. James is not afraid to share his faith with his fellow teachers or with the wider school community. There are good strong links between the school and the local church. The vicar is a member of the school governors and regularly takes assembly at the school.

Grace has a son called Christopher. Christopher attends the local primary school, and while Christopher is at school Grace works part-time in a local cafe. Grace meets a variety of people there, including local people and tourists. The work is tiring and sometimes very frustrating, but there are many opportunities to relate to people. Some of the regulars come in for a cup of tea and spend two or three hours in the cafe; some are shoppers wanting refreshment and a brief rest, some are passers-by who want the best service and in a hurry. What is interesting for Grace is that almost all want to talk about their lives. Over the years since working in the cafe, Grace has seen her vocation as a disciple of Christ to be to listen to these people. Grace listens to their stories, about their journeys, about their elderly parents who take a lot of their time, about their work and about their love lives.

Discipleship in daily life

The previous chapter looked at the call to Christian discipleship. This chapter looks at the call to be Christian disciples in daily life. How do people live out their discipleship in their working lives? Sometimes Christians have made a clear divide between what they do on Sundays at church and what they do the rest of the week. Work has been seen by some as something undertaken in order to create wealth and support the family, and by others as a way to gain social status or personal fulfilment.

TO DO

Reflect on your understanding of work.

- How do you understand work?
- Do you see a separation between what is done from Monday to Saturday and what is done on Sundays?
- How do you try to live out your discipleship in daily life?

From the creation of the world there has been some form of work. Ken Costa suggests that the paradigms for work are found in God's initiatives in creation and in the work of the Trinity. He argues that God laboured in creation and as stewards of that creation God expects people to work. He develops this by saying that 'God had the desire to create for us on earth the same attributes of sharing, service, partnership and collaboration that are enjoyed in the Godhead of Father, Son and Holy Spirit' (Costa, 2007, p. 18).

In talking about her secular vocation, Sue speaks of the creator God who brought the world into being and who continues to create. She is clear that her discipleship is very much part of what she does in her working life.

It is reasonable to assume from the New Testament that Jesus would have witnessed Joseph at work. As a carpenter Joseph would have balanced his working life alongside the demands of his Jewish faith. There is, however, no mention in the Scriptures of Jesus work-ing as a carpenter, either before his public ministry or after it had begun. In calling others to follow, some of his disciples were called to leave their fishing nets to follow him, but there are also examples of them continuing to fish. Certainly, he gave no general call for all Christians to give up everyday work and much of his teaching drew on themes from the world of everyday work. After Jesus' death, Paul emphasized a positive view of work, commending all Christians to continue in their work and to work well. Paul himself plainly continued in his trade as a tentmaker during his church-planting ministry, and this would seem to be the general Christian pattern for the first century after the apostles.

As Christianity grew and developed, the Church Fathers began to draw more heavily on Greek and Roman ideas in their theology and this more positive view of work gave way to a much lower view. This is reflected in the view of Eusebius who wrote about his doctrine of two lives about AD 300. He says:

> Two ways of life were thus given by the law of Christ to His Church. The one is above nature, and beyond common human living; it admits not marriage, child-bearing, property nor the posses-sion of wealth, but wholly and permanently separate from the common customary life of mankind, it devotes itself to the service of God alone ... such then is the perfect form of the Christian life. And the other, more humble, more human, permits man to join in pure nuptials, and to produce children ... it allows them to have minds for farming, for trade, and the other more secular interests as well as for religion ... a kind of secondary grade of piety is attributed to them. (www.worklife.org/worklife_articles/faithandworkarticle2.html)

In a similar way, Augustine distinguished between the 'active life' and the 'contemplative life'. While both kinds of life were good, and Augustine expressed praise for the work of farmers, craftspeople and merchants, the contemplative life was clearly of a higher order. While at times it may be necessary to follow the active life, wher-ever possible one should choose the other. The one life is loved, the other endured. Very soon it was this view that dominated Christian thinking, until only those people pursuing the contemplative life or a priestly role in the Church were said to have a truly 'religious' vocation.

The word 'calling' therefore became reserved for those holy people who felt called to separate themselves from everyday human activities and relationships in order to devote themselves to a life of prayer. Many monastic orders were founded during the medieval era. In the hierarchy of callings, priests came high, but monks and nuns came even higher. To spend your time in contemplative prayer – absorbed in the vision of God and lost in wonder, love and praise – that was the highest calling to which anyone could aspire.

The Reformation saw a shift to a more balanced approach to work and faith. The work of Martin Luther, the sixteenth-century Reformer, recovered a sense that all of life, including daily work, could be understood as a calling from God.

According to Luther, we respond to the call to love our neighbour by fulfilling the duties that are associated with our everyday work. Work is our call to serve. This work includes domestic and civic duties as well as our employment. Luther said we can only truly serve God in the midst of everyday circumstances and attempts to elevate the significance of the contemplative life are false. In fact it is the monastic life that has no true calling. It is an escape from the true obedience to which God calls us. Luther's view tended to defend the status quo socially and he had a fairly negative view of working for profit. John Calvin developed a more dynamic view that encouraged a greater degree of urban enterprise and the possibility of changing vocations. He identified a person's vocation more closely with their job (Mackenzie, 1997).

TO DO

In your experience, do you think that the call to ordained ministry or the religious life is a higher calling than the call to discipleship in everyday life? What has led to this view?

With the gradual decline of religious belief and practice people no longer worked in order to glorify God. Throughout the eighteenth and nineteenth centuries, religion declined and the process of secularization began; the worship of God and the call of God were gradually replaced simply by the duties and roles of society.

As society developed in a secularized way, the word 'vocation' survived but there was a gradual restriction in its application. As commercialism became stronger and it became clearer that many people in business were motivated principally by self-interest, rather than care for others, the language of calling came to seem less appropriate.

In church circles, the old medieval distinction between sacred and secular occupations reappeared, though in a slightly different form. Monks were no longer at the head of the list; missionaries were. They were followed by church leaders or people who worked full time for overtly Christian organizations. People might have a vocation to one or other of the so-called 'caring' professions: doctor, nurse, teacher, or social worker. Some might even have a calling to be politicians, but the idea of a calling to or vocation to other jobs, including the business world, disappeared from most people's understanding of the word 'vocation' (Higginson, 2002).

Secular vocation

Christianity in the early centuries of the Church concentrated on the general notion of being a Christian wherever a person happened to be in society. As far as can be seen, relatively little attention was given to helping individual Christians face the question of where God wanted them to be and what God wanted them to do in society. In other words, little help was given to people with a specific 'secular vocation' – that is, a vocation as a Christian centred upon daily life and work in the world.

In 1986 the Methodist Church produced a report called *The Ministry of the People of God*, in which section B2 looked at Christian ministries in daily life and work (Methodist Church, 2000, pp. 199–

202). In this section the word vocation is explored and the Methodist Church recognizes that Methodists have not normally followed classical Protestantism in using the vocabulary of 'vocation' to understand the role of people called to live out their faith in their daily work. Rather, the Methodist Church has in the past tended to connect the term vocation with an ordained person who is set apart in full-time pastoral charge.

The Methodist report goes on to discuss the idea of secular vocations and to affirm the enormous range of activities that can become 'for Christian people an authentic secular vocation'. The report emphasizes that those called to a secular vocation do so for the 'well-being of society and the natural order' and that the tasks undertaken are 'gladly performed for the glory of God' (p. 202).

Sue, James and Grace see their work as a secular vocation. Each has different gifts that they bring to their jobs and each uses these skills for the greater glory of God. As Sue works through the seasons of the year and watches the park gardens change from the death of autumn and winter to resurrection in spring and summer, she often finds herself reciting hymns reflecting the seasons and praising God for the goodness of God's creation.

James, too, finds himself praising God as he sees children develop and grow into what God wants them to be. As he reflects on his role, James recognizes the hand of God guiding him and his staff to nurture children for the well-being of society, and feels strongly that God has called him to this role in society.

Grace acknowledges that she could move into a more high-powered job now that Christopher is at school, but in her secular vocation she feels that God has put her in the cafe to be a listening ear for those who need someone to listen to them. Grace feels that in her job she offers people a place to be, a place to rest and a place of community.

Lay discipleship

The Church of England uses the terminology of lay disciples rather than secular vocations. In 1983, through the General Synod's Board of Education, it set up a working group to look at the theology of the laity. Its conclusions were published in 1985 in the document *All Are Called* (Church of England Board of Education, 1985). In 1987 a follow-up document was published, *Called to Be Adult Disciples* (Church of England Board of Education, 1987). Both reports called on the Church to value and affirm the discipleship of all lay people, and especially those whose call was specifically focused on their everyday life of work, home and leisure. The first report states:

> Because all human beings are made in the image of God, they are called to become the People of God, the Church, servants and ministers and citizens of the Kingdom, a new humanity in Jesus Christ. Though we are tainted by our sinfulness, God's wonderful grace and love offer us all this common Christian vocation. God leaves everyone free to refuse this call; but the call is there for all without exception. The young are called; the elderly are called. There is no retirement from the Christian pilgrimage. The beautiful are called, and also the unlovely. The sick are called as well as the healthy and the energetic. Activists are called and also quiet people. We are called regardless of our intellectual abilities or our formal education. We are called regardless of our race or nationality or social class. (Church of England Board of Education, 1985, p. 3)

A decade or so later, a working group of the Church of England's Board of Education produced a report, *Called to New Life: The World of Lay Discipleship* (Archbishops' Council, 1999). This report used the work of a group of businessmen from the Diocese of Peterborough to reflect on lay people and the Church. It built up a picture of the skills and gifts that lay disciples bring to the Church, as a great diversity of 'talents, convictions, professions, attitudes, pastimes, and responsibilities' (p. 15).

The report also looks at the ways in which dioceses within the Church of England responded to the idea of linking faith and life. It reports on the appointment of adult education advisers and how they have tried to develop courses for people to reflect on how they live out their discipleship in the world. It also explores the various organizations that have developed to support people in their daily work. These organizations include Christians in Public Life, Industry Churches Forum and the Ridley Hall Foundation.

In the chapter 'Fruit of the Cross', the report sets out an understanding of what it is to be lay disciples both in the Church and in the world. It becomes clear that for many lay people making the distinction between the Church and the world is a false division and 'does not ring true'. The two are intimately related, because the Church is always in the world. These are certainly the feelings of Sue, James and Grace, since they clearly see their vocation in their daily life as intrinsically connected to their worship on Sundays and their commitment to the Church.

Called to New Life also suggests that:

> The laity have certain responsibilities and duties, given to them by God as revealed by Jesus Christ. The focus of the lay life is in the world. It is in the ordinary conditions of daily life in which lay people find themselves that the duties of faith, hope, love and charity are expressed. It is primarily in streets and neighbourhoods, at work, in the school playground and supermarkets that lay people respond to their vocation as Christians as well as in the church. (p. 42)

Sue, James and Grace live out their duties as Christians in various ways, and not just in their workplace. For Sue, the gym is another place where she lives out her calling as she seeks refreshment and renewal from her daily life. For James, it is in a night class where he learns and engages with others. For Grace, it's in the playground as she engages with the other mums and dads.

TO DO

Where in your everyday life do you see your call to discipleship expressed?

Do others know that you are a follower of Christ? If so, how? How does that reflect your calling?

Since *Called to New Life* was published, other organizations have developed to help people in their discipleship within daily life. One such organization is called After Sunday, which began in 2005 as a project supported by the Mission Fund of the Diocese of Durham. Its aim is to help Christians strengthen the connection that they make between faith, work and the world. Their website has this to say about its aims:

After Sunday promotes an integrated approach to faith, life and work whilst recognizing the challenges posed by a complex and fragmented world. After Sunday encourages a focus on work as one of the most important and testing contexts in which people need to make stronger connections and respond to the activity of God in the world. From an After Sunday viewpoint the word 'work' can also embrace any purposeful creative human engagement whether paid, voluntary, caring, housework, unwaged, self-employed, studying, retired etc. This includes most people at whatever stage they are at in their lives. After Sunday encourages a holistic view of church as being a community that gathers together for worship, learning and support, as well as being a community that is dispersed into the world to 'be' the church in service and responding to God's activity and call. After Sunday is not setting out to be an alternative form of church. Rather After Sunday seeks to act as a bridge and focus for unity in the church. It has been set up to be independent of any particular denomination or institution. After Sunday is neither particularly conservative nor liberal in its approach. Rather it encourages a radical and direct engagement in the challenging issues of life. In so doing, it encourages people to explore faithful and hopeful responses to God's calling. (www.afterchurchsunday.org.uk)

Another organization that has worked to reflect on the role of discipleship in daily life is the Ridley Hall Foundation through its Faith in Business project (www.ridley.cam.ac.uk/centres/faith-in-business), which began in 1989 with the original title God on Monday Project. Faith in Business is a project concerned with relating Christian faith to the world of work, notably that of business. It developed to counter the Churches' concept of lay ministry, which was felt to be too often restricted to what lay people can do for the Church, rather than taking in lay people's work that occupies most of their time.

The project is concerned with faith in business in a twofold way: affirming the role of business in God's purposes and exploring the application of Christian faith and values in business. It seeks to encourage lay Christians to be faithful disciples in demanding working contexts.

TO DO

Which of the projects about faith and work have you come across and explored?

Look at the website for either After Sunday or the Ridley Hall Foundation and, drawing on your own experience, reflect on the ways that such a project could help people foster their vocation to discipleship in the workplace.

The director of Faith in Business, Richard Higginson, has explored the issues of discipleship in business in his book, *Questions of Business Life: Exploring Workplace Issues from a Christian Perspective*. He writes:

The final lesson to heed about work as vocation is to remember that it is a secondary vocation. The Protestant Reformers taught this, but as we have seen, their teaching got distorted in the centuries that followed. The primary vocation is to heed the call of Jesus and follow him. Work should be seen in the overall context of discipleship. We are called to serve and honour God with every fibre of our being, in all areas of life: family, local or wider community and leisure pursuits, as well as the work which takes up most of our time and the church which too easily becomes the dominating focus of our 'Christian' activity. Vocation needs to be integrated into an all-embracing understanding about God's claim on the whole of our lives. (Higginson, 2002, pp. 138–9)

Sue, James and Grace certainly feel that the call to follow is evidenced in the whole of their lives. Like many, they have had difficulty in getting the Church to understand this call to the whole of life and not just to authorized ministries within the Church. They recognize that the situation is improving and have welcomed the Church of England's document, *Shaping the Future* (Archbishops' Council, 2006).

In their churches, education for discipleship programmes are beginning to take shape with the recognition that discipleship is the term used to describe 'the whole life-response of Christians to Jesus Christ'.

Conclusion

This chapter has explored the call to discipleship in everyday life. It has looked at the historical development of the idea of work and how the understanding of work and discipleship has changed through the centuries. It has explored how the Methodist Church and the Anglican Church have over the past 30 years tried to resource lay people in their everyday lives. It has also explored the work of organizations who have tried to overcome the divide between the Church and work.

Further reading

Church of England Board of Education, 1987, *Called to be Adult Disciples*, London: Church House Publishing.

Costa, K., 2007, *God at Work: Living Every Day with Purpose*, London: Continuum.

Higginson, R., 2002, *Questions of Business Life: Exploring Workplace Issues from a Christian Perspective*, London: Spring Harvest.

Richardson, C. (ed.), 2004, *This is Our Calling*, London: SPCK.

Torry, M. (ed.), 2006, *Diverse Gifts*, Norwich: Canterbury Press.

5

Called to a Variety of Lay Ministries

Introduction

This chapter begins by listening to how Christian lay ministers discuss their vocations and ministries. Particular attention is given to the expression of four individuals: a lay pastoral assistant, a lay worship leader, a lay street pastor and a lay children's minister. These accounts are set in conversation with the ways in which the Churches discuss the theology and practice of such ministries, and test vocations to such ministries and offer training for them. This chapter is designed to help us to assess our own sense of call and vocation to lay ministries.

Introducing Bob, Rowan, Maggie and Kath

Bob has just retired from the local hospital, where he has been a porter for the past 25 years. He has always been a loyal member of the local church, but found very little time to commit himself fully. As retirement drew near, Bob felt called to use the skills he had gained in his working life for the service of the Church. He approached his vicar and told him that he felt God was calling him to work in the Church as a lay person. After training on the local education for discipleship course, Bob has been licensed as a pastoral assistant and spends three days a week visiting the housebound and taking people to hospital for their appointments. Bob is part of a team of people who offer pastoral care to the local community as well as to the church community. Although Bob's ministry of pastoral care is directed both to the church community and to the local community, other people in the team offer pastoral care primarily to the church community. Bob's wider experience in the hospital gives him the ability to work closely with the caring agencies in the community.

Rowan is a deputy headteacher at the local secondary school. He teaches music at the school and has conducted the very successful school choir. Rowan became a Christian at university partly through singing with a cathedral choir and partly through the university chaplaincy. Rowan believes that it was through the cathedral music and choruses sung at the chaplaincy that he came to Christian faith and felt able to demonstrate and share his faith with others.

Rowan plays the organ at church, which is a lively church with a variety of lay ministries and a commitment to shared ministry. Over the past few years his role has developed from organist to parish musician and he now feels called to the ministry of worship leader. This call comes as a result of leading worship in school over the past year. Rowan has approached the minister and talked through his call.

Maggie is a solicitor who spends her working life dealing with young offenders who have got into trouble through alcohol and drug abuse. She is also a committed member of the local Anglican church and has felt called to work with young people through the church. There is in her area a very active group of churches who work together ecumenically. When this group of churches decided to launch the Street Pastor initiative in the locality, Maggie felt that God was calling her to this ministry. Maggie undertook training before being commissioned with a group of local church people to work on the streets of her town on a Friday and Saturday evening. Maggie has a street pastor partner with whom she works and they walk the streets offering help and support to youngsters who may have had too much to drink or are under the influence of other substances. They offer a listening ear and the practical support of water and flip-flops. Maggie's training is ongoing, but she feels that she is where God wants her to be; she feels that God walks with her as she visits the pubs to talk with the young people.

Kath is a young mum with two children. She began attending church regularly just before the baptism of her first child. Kath had gone to Sunday school when she was growing up and remembers some of the Bible stories she was taught as a child. In her working life she is a children's nurse and feels called to work with children through the Church. Her church is a 'new church' on a relatively new housing estate where there are a number of young families. Kath meets many of the young mums at the baby clinic she attends with her own children and discerns a need for young families to meet, talk and socialize. As Kath's faith grows, she feels that God is calling her to work with these young families through the church and to offer them the opportunity to come together to share their experience of raising children and of family life. In discussion with her church leaders, Kath sets up a baby and toddler group which brings together young children and mums, grandparents and carers. Health professionals visit the group and all sessions end with a short service. As the group has grown, Kath has found herself called, with others in the church, to develop a ministry among children and young people.

The group of children's workers that has emerged hold strongly to the view that children should be nurtured in faith alongside and with other members of the congregation. They believe that they are all pilgrims in faith, and consequently Kath has developed a service of all-age worship once a month.

As children's ministry develops, Kath recognizes that she and the people who work with her need more training. They need to know about how faith develops and is learned, as well as about faith-related issues such as those around suffering.

TO DO

What experiences do you have of any of the ministries discussed above?

Reflecting on your experience, what value is there in these different types of lay ministry?

Lay ministry

Chapter 3 looked at the call to discipleship and the idea that from discipleship flows ministry. Peter Edwards (2004) suggests that it is the role of the whole people of God to participate in worship, service and mission. He goes on to argue that this is what the Church is for and that within the 'divinely established and led institution and community, there are also individual ministries for members' (p. 101) as their discipleship develops. Lay ministry has grown and developed over the past 40 years. This is due only in part to the falling number of ordained clergy; it is also due to the growing theological conviction across all Churches that ministry is the responsibility of the whole people of God (Church of England, 2007a).

The Lima report stated:

> The Holy Spirit bestows on the community diverse and complementary gifts. These are for the common good of the whole people and are manifested in acts of service within the community and the world. They may be gifts of communicating the Gospel in word and deed, gifts of healing, gifts of praying, gifts of teaching and learning, gifts of serving, gifts of guiding and following, gifts of inspiration and vision. All members are called to discover, with the help of the community, the gifts they have received and to use them for the building up of the church and the service of the world to which the church is sent. (World Council of Churches, 1982, p. 20)

By the end of the twentieth century a large number of different forms of lay ministry had developed. Within the Anglican Church some of these ministries have been developed and recognized at national level, some at diocesan level and others at parochial level. This chapter looks at four particular lay ministries to which people have felt called: the ministries of pastoral assistant, worship leader, street pastor, and the ministry to children.

Pastoral assistants

Pastoral assistants are those in whom the Church has discerned special gifts for 'pastoral care in the church and wider community'. Peter Griffiths (2006), in the edited book *Diverse Gifts: Varieties of Lay and Ordained Ministries in the Church and Community*, has written a chapter on the development of pastoral assistants from his experience in the Diocese of Southwark. This ministry began over 40 years ago in the diocese and was called Southwark Pastoral Auxiliary (SPA).

The vision for SPAs was that of Cecilia Goodenough, who was the assistant to the diocesan missioner. Cecilia used her social services background to promote and develop this ministry. There was a strong emphasis on training. The early trainees attended lectures on doctrine and ethics, and undertook biblical studies in small groups. This was undertaken while trainees worked in the community.

This ministry has developed over the past 40 years, and the Diocese of Southwark continues to train people for pastoral ministry. The diocesan website reported in 2011:

> Southwark Pastoral Auxiliaries (SPAs) are lay men and women authorised by the Diocese to help develop caring and pastoral work on behalf of the church, in a voluntary capacity. At present there are about 190 active SPAs in the Diocese. (www.southwark.anglican.org/ministry/southwark-pastoral-auxiliary-ministry)

The Diocese of Southwark believes that SPAs are called to help put God's caring concern for all people into practice. They do this:

- through their own direct contact with people;
- by encouraging and enabling others to exercise a caring ministry;
- by raising awareness of pastoral care needs within their local church and neighbourhood.

In the Diocese of Southwark there are a variety of ways in which SPA ministry is expressed, there is not one definitive description for a pastoral worker. Some SPAs work mainly within their local church;

others work mainly within the local community, based in a local caring agency or project. These two different ways of SPA ministry may converge and there may be a mix of the two within one person's ministry. There is also some flexibility surrounding this type of ministry as the focus of each SPA's ministry will vary in accordance with the needs within their local church and community, and in accordance with their own gifts, experience, knowledge and interests.

Within the diocese SPAs are representatives of the Church who work towards the task of building up a society that is both caring and just. They encourage and develop the pastoral care offered by the whole people of God.

The Diocese of Chelmsford has also developed the ministry of pastoral assistants. Its website states that pastoral assistants 'are not people who know all the answers'. They are men and women of prayer; people who reflect on the dilemmas of modern life in the light of the Bible and Christian tradition; and people who want to communicate to others the message of Christ through caring action. They are people who are willing to develop creatively their abilities in teamwork, leadership, listening and caring. Pastoral assistants are those with pastoral gifts who will exercise a leadership role in this ministry, acting as an example and encouraging others to use their gifts (www.chelmsford.anglican.org/pastoral-assistants.html).

In the Diocese of Chelmsford pastoral assistants have a variety of roles, including:

- healing and wholeness;
- supporting the sick and bereaved;
- hospital, prison, industrial and other chaplaincies;
- working with caring agencies in the wider community;
- assisting with occasional offices;
- co-ordinating a pastoral care team;
- collaborating with clergy and other ministers;
- pastoral visiting and support.

In his diocese, Bob's calling to pastoral ministry is to care pastorally for those both inside and outside the Church. Bob has chosen to do this because he feels that his experience in his working life has given him the skills to do so.

Bob has a number of roles within the team of pastoral assistants. He enjoys pastoral visiting and offering support to those who are sick and to the homeless. He works within a team of people who fulfil some of the other roles described by the Diocese of Chelmsford. He feels strongly that the training he has received for this role within the Church, and his work experience in the hospital, give him the skills and gifts to serve God in this way. He feels very much part of a team.

TO DO

What is your experience of pastoral assistants?

Are you aware of the ministry in your local churches?

What benefits do they bring to the Church?

Worship leaders

Worship leaders within the Church have historically been seen as those who guide the congregation in singing. This may well have been the traditional choirmaster or choirmistress. As the numbers of clergy and ministers have declined, the Church has broadened this understanding to include people who lead worship. The term 'worship leader' is now used to refer to the person who leads the congregation in its devotions as a whole.

In the Diocese of Europe, congregational worship leaders are authorized to lead Morning or Evening Prayer or other services that comply with the *Common Worship* provisions of a Service of the Word. They are not authorized to preach or to preside at pastoral offices, although sermons or homilies prepared by or approved by the incumbent may be read. In certain situations a congregational worship leader may be given additional authorization to conduct funerals, after the archdeacon is satisfied that he or she has been given suitable training by the incumbent for this work (www.europe. anglican.org).

The Diocese of Sheffield has worship leaders and provides training for them. The aims of the training course are to:

- nurture the growth of personal worship as foundational;
- lead others effectively in worship;
- provide a biblical and historical background to worship;
- provide a broad understanding of current worship styles across the church traditions;
- develop new expertise and practical skills. (www.sheffield.anglican.org/.../church...worship/worship-4-today)

Rowan has in the past been responsible for the choir in the church, but his experience of sacred music has developed to include different styles of worship. Rowan is part of a team of people responsible for worship, who have worked hard to lead others effectively in worship. They have studied the historical and theological background to worship and with their knowledge of music they have a valuable ministry within their church. Their minister has very little musical background and so welcomes their input and expertise. The minister recognizes that God has given people different gifts in order to serve God, and works with the worship group to produce good and creative worship.

TO DO

What is your experience of worship leaders?

Are you aware of their ministry in your local churches?

What benefits do they bring to the Church?

Street pastors

The ministry of a street pastor is a relatively new ministry in the Church. The inspiration behind the ministry of street pastors came from Revd Les Isaac of the Ascension Trust, who launched the Street Pastor Scheme in April 2003. His aim was to patrol the streets and connect with the community, particularly with young people who feel excluded.

> A Street Pastor is a Church leader or member with a concern for society – in particular young people who feel themselves to be excluded and marginalised – and who is willing to engage people where they are, in terms of their thinking (i.e. their perspective of life) and location, where they hang out – be it on the streets, in the pubs and clubs or at parties. (www.streetpastors.org.uk)

Maggie feels called to this type of ministry and to use her experience as a solicitor to help young people. She feels called to engage with young people before they get to court. Maggie is able to bring her knowledge of young people in her working life to bear as she walks the streets of her local area and engages in conversations with young people.

Street pastors will also be willing to work with fellow activists, church and community leaders, and with both statutory and voluntary agencies and projects, to look at collaborative ways of working on issues affecting youth and initiatives that will build trust between them and the street pastors. Maggie's work brings her into contact with many young people's agencies and projects, and she consequently feels able to engage with them through her ministry as a street pastor.

Les Isaac believes that as street pastors get to know people in the community they will find out what their needs are and what can be done to help. A presence of street pastors will earn credibility in the community, so that people know that the Church is there for them in a practical way. Here is a ministry of listening, caring and helping – working in an unconditional way.

Those offering themselves as street pastors undergo training, including training offered by the police. The police teach the street pastors about crowd control, anger management and police protocol. The initiative is a collaborative partnership between local authorities, the police and the churches. Street pastors like Maggie will have undergone 12 days training over a five-month period before being allowed to patrol the streets.

The work of the street pastors has been praised both by the police and also in a recent Home Office report, *Tackling Knife Crime Together*, by actress Brooke Kinsella (Kinsella, 2011) whose brother Ben was stabbed and killed in 2008. The street pastors initiative is cited as a good example of street-based work.

It is also a good example of churches coming together to offer a service to the local community. Maggie has met many different street pastors from different churches in her vicinity. She has been able to put her working experience to good use for the service of the Church, and Maggie feels supported by the local churches as they pray for and work with the street pastors.

TO DO

Do you know of people who are working as street pastors?

What do you think is the gospel message shown through this type of ministry?

Children's minister

Ministry among children has developed over a longer period of time than the previous two lay ministries. The Church's role in children's formal education goes back to its work with schools in the nineteenth century. At the beginning of this century, Lord Dearing (2001), in his report *The Way Ahead: Church of England Schools in the New Millennium*, has highlighted the potential for creative relationships between parish church and school.

Ministry among children and young people, whether in school or in church, is built upon a theology of creation: God created human beings in the image of God. This means that all people whatever their age are complete human beings (Archbishops' Council Education Division, 2010). The Church's task is to model and teach what it means for all Christians on their journey of faith, whether they be young children or mature adults.

Over the past 40 years the Church has produced a number of reports highlighting the importance of work among children. Much of this thinking about children and the Church comes from the report *The Child in the Church*, produced by the British Council of Churches (1976). The key concept developed by the *Child in the Church* was the notion of Christian nurture (see Francis and Astley, 2002, chs 7 and 9). The report states:

> We understand Christian nurture first of all when we see that it springs out of the nature of the Christian life itself as a process of continuous growth. The growth does not take place in isolation, but in the company with others who are also working in the same way. Our understanding of nature is thus bound up with our understanding of the Church, the community of the way. (British Council of Churches, 1976, p. 19)

This is an understanding that Kath holds, although she may not have articulated it in the same way. As a child Kath felt nurtured by the person who led her Sunday school, but she also recognizes that this nurture ceased when she became a teenager. Kath believes that she is called to nurture children from a very young age and that nurture takes place in the company of others, both lay and ordained.

Twelve years after the publication of *The Child in the Church*, the Church of England published the report *Children in the Way* (Church of England, 1988). As its starting point it takes the following quotation from *The Child in the Church* report:

> The church that does not accept children unconditionally in its fellowship is depriving those children of what is rightfully theirs,

but the deprivation such as the Church itself will suffer is far more grave. (Church of England, 1988, p. 1)

The report then develops two models, which have become central to an Anglican understanding of ministry among children and young people. The first model is that of the pilgrim church. A pilgrim church is a church in which adults and children travel together, learn from one another and in which sometimes children lead the way. The second model is that of all-age worship. In the pilgrim church opportunities are given for adults and children to worship together. By virtue of their baptism, the report states, children are full and equal partners on the faith journey.

Kath has recognized in her ministry the need for people to travel together regardless of age. She now helps the minister once a month to prepare an all-age worship service where all ages of the church worship together. What Kath sees, when adults and children worship together, is nurture both of children and adults. She observes how both age groups learn about the Kingdom of God from each other (see Francis and Astley, 2002, ch. 28).

A further report, *All God's Children*, published by the Church of England (1991b) highlighted the issue of low numbers of children having contact with the local church. It suggested that Sunday may not be the best day to reach unchurched children. This was true for Kath, who finds that more people attend the mid-week mother and toddlers group than the all-age worship service. In her church the minister and those working with children have decided to have mid-week worship as well as Sunday worship in order to cater for the different family commitments.

Over ten years later the Church of England published a report, *Sharing the Good News with Children: The Church of England's Children's Strategy* (Church of England, 2003). This report builds on previous reports and highlights four key areas:

- worship and nurture of children;
- children and evangelism;
- supporting ministry among children;
- training for ministry among children.

Further reports that have been produced include *Children in the Midst* (2005a) and *Children Included* (2005b). These papers develop the fourth key area from *Sharing the Good News with Children* (2003): training for a ministry among children. They advocate training programmes for clergy, readers and those lay people directly involved in children's ministry. Kath is keen to use her skills of child development to learn more about the spiritual development of children and young people. She is keen to use the Core Skills Programme developed by the Consultative Group on Ministry among Children (CGMC, 2006) to increase her knowledge, and the other workers' knowledge, of working with children in a Christian context.

TO DO

Reflect on your own experience of ministry among children and young people.

Have you any experience of programmes to train people for ministry among children?

Why do you think it is important to educate children's workers, and in what areas?

Conclusion

This chapter has explored how people have used their skills and gifts to minister in the Church. It has explored the role of pastoral assistants, worship leaders, street pastors and children's ministers. These ministries are set in the context of the ministry of the *laos*, the whole people of God. In the New Testament various ministries can be seen emerging in the early Church, including the ministries of healing, preaching, teaching and caring. God gives many diverse gifts to people. In this chapter, although space has permitted only four ministries of the laity to be discussed, it is recognized that God calls us into discipleship through baptism and gives different gifts to different people in order to serve God and God's Kingdom.

Further reading

Bowden, A. and West, M., 2000, *Dynamic Local Ministry*, London: Continuum.

Church of England, 2005a, *Children in the Midst*, London: Church House Publishing.

Dewar, F., 2000, *Called or Collared?*, London: SPCK.

Francis, L. J. and Astley, J. (eds), 2002, *Children, Churches and Christian Learning*, London: SPCK.

Richardson, C. (ed.), 2004, *This Is Our Calling*, London: SPCK.

Torry. M. (ed.), 2006, *Diverse Gifts: Varieties of Lay and Ordained Ministries in the Church Community*, Norwich: Canterbury Press.

6

Called to Reader and Local Preacher Ministry

Introduction

This chapter begins by listening to the experiences of ordinary Christians in respect of two lay ministries experienced across the Anglican and Methodist Churches. These accounts are then set in conversation with the historic understandings of authorized ministries in the two denominations. Particular attention is given to ministry leadership in the Anglican and Methodist Churches. This chapter is designed to help us to assess our own sense of call and vocation to lay ministries in today's Church.

Introducing Janet and Graham

Janet is a Reader in her local Anglican church. She lives in a remote multi-parish benefice in the Lake District. A number of years ago she agreed to lead morning worship in the parish church when the incumbent could not get there. As her confidence grew, Janet felt the gentle nudge of God and offered herself for Reader ministry. In order to undertake this function, Janet had to go through a formal process of discernment and selection. Once she was selected she had to undertake a two-year programme of training to be a Reader. The main part of her job is taking services of Morning Prayer and Evening Prayer in a number of local churches in her area. Janet feels called to this ministry in order to preach and teach the faith. Janet works at the local supermarket and many of the local people know her as the Reader at the local church. In her role as Reader, Janet takes services at which she preaches. Janet also has a teaching ministry and in her local church people meet together to learn more about their faith.

Five years ago Graham felt God calling him to be a Local Preacher in his local Methodist church; he had been attending church all his life and from time to time had benefited from the ministry of Local Preachers and felt that God was calling him to live out his vocation as a postman and as a Local Preacher. Graham informed his minister that he was sure God was calling him to Local Preacher ministry. After their initial talk, Graham spoke to the superintendent of the Methodist circuit who put him in touch with the Local Preachers' Meeting. After a period of assessment and training, Graham was admitted as a Local Preacher in a service of admission for Local Preachers. Graham enjoys his ministry and the local people know him as both their postman and their preacher. Graham leads worship and preaches in his local circuit at least twice a month.

TO DO

What is your experience of people who are not ordained but lead and preach at services?

How are these services different from ones led by ordained ministers?

Reader ministry in the Anglican Church

The office of Reader in the Church of England began in its present form in the second half of the nineteenth century. The first steps came as a result of a meeting of the Convention of Canterbury in the 1850s, when a committee was established to explore the possibility of reviving the order of Reader. The decision was taken to do so at a meeting of the archbishops and bishops at Lambeth Palace on Ascension Day 1866.

In 1866 the recommendations of this meeting were implemented and lay people could be licensed to Reader ministry in the Church. There were appropriate safeguards as these first Readers could resign at any time and the bishop could revoke their commission if it was found that a Reader was preaching heresy or was not of good character (Rowling and Gooder, 2009).

At this time Reader ministry was agreed across the whole of the Church of England, in the Province of Canterbury and the Province of York. The rationale behind the revival was largely as a means to extend the effectiveness of the traditional parochial system to new pioneering work on the boundaries between Church and world.

At the beginning, the role of the Reader in services was limited to reading lessons at Morning and Evening Prayer (but not at Holy Communion) and saying the Litany. The role of the Reader has since evolved. In 1884 Readers were allowed to lead Morning and Evening Prayer, but they could not preach in a consecrated building (Rowling and Gooder, 2009). In 1941 Readers were allowed to read the Epistle but not the Gospel; to administer the chalice but not the paten; and to preach at Morning and Evening Prayer from the chancel steps, but not at Holy Communion. In 1969 Readers were authorized to read the Gospel and to preach at Holy Communion, and Reader ministry was extended to women as well as to men. Ten years later, in 1979, Readers were allowed to conduct funeral services. In 1988 Readers were given permission to administer the consecrated elements of Holy Communion as part of their licence.

In those early days selection of potential Readers was simple: to become a Reader the bishop needed assurance that the person was of moral character and had some knowledge of the Christian faith and the Scriptures. In 1904 there appears to be two categories of Readers, parochial Readers and diocesan Readers, the distinction between them being their educational attainment. Parochial Readers were less adequately trained and ministered in poorer churches, while the diocesan Readers were more adequately trained or had been professionally trained. It was a distinction that remained until 1941, when new regulations stated that all Readers were to be licensed in the same way to hold office.

Today Reader ministry is publicly authorized with an oath to the bishop and legally supported with the bishop's licence. *Reader Upbeat* (Church of England, 2008) suggests that this public authorization is a sign of the Church's ministry in the world and that it is that part of God's action that is expressed through the Church.

Before gaining a bishop's licence to be a Reader, a candidate will undergo selection and training. Janet, having worked as a worship leader for a number of years, felt the call to Reader ministry. Following a conversation, her incumbent suggested that she speak with the person responsible for Reader ministry in the diocese. Having spoken with this warden of Readers, Janet became aware that the selection of Readers was quite rigorous and that there are now specific selection criteria that need to be fulfilled if she was to become a Reader. These criteria fall under eight headings (Church of England, 1998):

- Ministry in the Church of England
- Vocation
- Faith
- Spirituality and worship
- Personality and character
- Relationships
- Potential for training
- Leadership and collaboration.
  (For a fuller description, see www.readers.cofe.anglican.org/u_d_lib_pub/p152.pdf)

Once candidates have been selected for training for Reader ministry, they begin an in-depth training course. Both the scope and rigour of Reader training developed very considerably during the second half of the twentieth century. Before 1946 Readers were usually licensed on the basis of a recommendation to the bishop. A national examination was introduced for the first time in 1946, which gradually increased in scope and became the 'General Reader's Examination'. In 1975 this was replaced by an essay scheme, for which reading lists were provided, and a 'General Reader's Certificate' (GRC) was awarded on the basis of 16 assessed essays based on specific sections of the syllabus. Only a quarter of those admitted as Readers, however, obtained a GRC. From 1989 the centralized scheme was abandoned and each diocese became responsible for devising and delivering its own Reader training course, subject to oversight through a system of national moderation.

Formation for Ministry within a Learning Church (Archbishops' Council, 2003) placed its ministerial education and formation of clergy in the context of the overall provision for ministerial training, lay training and formal lay adult education and from this a group was formed to look at Reader ministry in particular. The document *Shaping the Future* (Archbishops' Council, 2006) suggested that Reader ministry training should be shaped by three interlinking areas: knowledge and understanding, competence, and conviction.

When Jane began her Reader training, she was instructed to keep the three areas in balance. Under the heading of knowledge and understanding Jane learned about the Bible, the doctrines of the Church, and liturgy and worship. Under the heading of competence, she learned how to lead worship, preach, teach, be a good communicator and how to engage in an appropriate way in pastoral situations. Under the last heading of competence and conviction, Janet learned how to nurture her Christian life and ministry through developing and reflecting on her commitment to personal prayer and to public worship. She also learned to reflect on other ways of worshipping God and how different spiritualities enable people to relate to God in different ways.

After two years of training, Janet was licensed by her bishop as a Reader. In the 2006 service for the admission and licensing of Readers in the Church of England's *Common Worship*, the following words of commission are used:

> My brothers and sisters, God has gathered us into the fellowship of the universal Church. As members together of his body, Christ calls us to minister in his name and, according to our gifts, to be instruments of his love in the world. Within this ministry, Readers are called to serve the Church of God and to work together with clergy and other ministers. They are to lead public worship, to

preach and teach the word of God, to assist at the Eucharist and to share in pastoral and evangelistic work. As authorized lay ministers, they are to encourage the ministries of God's people, as the Spirit distributes gifts among us all. They are called to help the whole Church to participate in God's mission to the world. (www. churchofengland.org/media/41172/admissionrederspdf)

Janet was licensed to work with the clergy and other lay ministers and to serve the Church. Pat Nappin (2002) suggests that the role of the Reader is to act as a bridge, between lay and ordained, between the Church and the world, between the world of work and the home, and between individual members of the church family.

In her ministry as a Reader, Janet certainly sees her role as a bridge. In her work at the supermarket people stop and talk to her about issues of faith and the Church; she feels that she naturally bridges the gap between the world of work and the home, and between the Church and the world.

Some people have asked her to take funerals because they know Janet and can relate to her. The relationships that Janet has built up because of her work enables her to get close to people both in the ordinary times of life and in the distressing times.

One of the roles of a Reader is to preach and Readers may have the opportunity to preach regularly. They are able to preach both within and outside the body of the Church. They have their experience of being part of the worshipping Church, but also part of the world. Readers can and do bring to the Church an awareness of worldly affairs from daily life and many different spheres.

Janet certainly feels that in her preaching she can and does bring in the needs of the world and of her particular community, as she sees them from the perspective of her daily life. Janet spends time reflecting on how the many situations she encounters at work can be used to illustrate sermons.

Readers are also involved in a teaching ministry and Janet is part of a local education group in her church where she facilitates the learning of others. The group meets weekly to discuss what they have read from a particular textbook on the given subject being studied. Janet enjoys this part of being a Reader as she feels that she learns from others in the discussion group.

Readers have an important liturgical role. They may lead Morning and Evening Prayer, they may lead the ministry of the word in the Eucharist service, they may take funeral services, and they may lead all-age worship and informal services. Readers may also administer the elements at a service of Holy Communion and some take communion to those who are housebound.

In her ministry Janet spends more time taking Morning and Evening Prayer at her local church, but she now helps out at Holy Communion at the major Christian festivals, which she feels is a real privilege.

TO DO

Reflect on your experience of Reader ministry.

- Do you think that Readers are used to their full capabilities?
- How easy is it for Readers to be seen as an extension of the clergy?

Local Preachers in the Methodist Church

Methodist lay preachers have been part of the Methodist Church since its inception. Margaret Batty, in an edited book called *Workaday Preachers* (Milburn and Batty, 1995), recounts stories of two of the original lay preachers, Thomas Westell and Thomas Maxfield. Both preachers were allowed to preach by John and Charles Wesley, although the Wesleys had reservations because of the difficulties they themselves already faced as members of the Church of England. Other clergy in the Church of England saw the Wesleys as 'irregular' because they preached outdoors. Now the Wesleys had to deal with other 'irregularites' in their own movement, as unordained persons began to preach.

Opposition grew to lay people preaching, largely expressed through pamphlets. John and Charles Wesley continued to have their doubts, as they held a High Anglican view of the office of an ordained cleric within the Church. The needs of the Church to save souls eventually persuaded them, however, and in one of John Wesley's letters he says that he 'tolerates lay preaching' because if he did not many souls would be lost (Telford, 1931, p. 186).

The clergy of the Church of England objected to lay preachers on the grounds that they were uneducated. Charles Wesley's fear was that the use of lay preachers would precipitate the separation of Methodists from the Church of England. The success of these lay preachers, however, encouraged the Wesleys to continue to use them, and by 1740 the work of lay preachers was becoming more organized.

In an effort to organize the Methodist movement, the country was divided into 'rounds', now known as circuits, and men who were good preachers in their own area were called, employed and paid as full-time professional travelling preachers who took spiritual charge of a round. They worked through the round systematically over a period of four to six weeks, and every two years or less John Wesley moved them on.

At this time there was very little distinction between local preachers and travelling preachers. The requirements for both preachers were grace, a personal love of God that was reflected in the life of the preacher's behaviour, gifts of sound understanding, right judgement and the ability to speak so that the hearers could understand. In fact Wesley reported that as long as these marks were found in a person they were able to preach.

As Methodism developed so did the number of preachers. In the minutes of meetings held from 1751 onwards it becomes evident that local preachers were very much part of Methodism, although there was no formulated expression of the office of Local Preacher. Milburn and Batty (1995) suggest that (judging by the Minutes of Conference, Wesley's Journal, Letters and the lives of the early Methodist preachers) little was said specifically about local preachers in the first 25 years of Methodism, because in Wesley's eyes they were just preachers who were not travelling.

As Methodism grew and increased rapidly in numbers, the need to have structures in place became evident. The lack of control over lay preachers then became a problem and Wesley began to rein them in. It is interesting that in the Deed of Declaration of 1784, Wesley's will for Methodism, he did not give local preachers a place. Yet they continued to work as preachers and to build chapels. It was not until 1796 that Conference established the Local Preachers' Meeting. This meeting gave security to the circuits, because now there was a frequent check on the standards of preaching and security to the preacher, because the preacher's peers as well as the superintendent were now together to be the judges of his fitness to preach (Milburn and Batty, 1995).

The place of Local Preachers in the Church has always been important because they have served in areas of significant need, especially where ordained preachers were unable or unwilling to serve. As the ministry developed, Local Preachers were trained and the words used over two centuries ago continue today. The training talked about being 'on note', where the pupil would learn from an experienced preacher. Then followed a period 'on trial', at the end of which the preacher would conduct a whole act of worship, preach a trial sermon before his or her peers and undergo an oral examination before preachers to test his or her required knowledge of 'our doctrines' and Wesley's sermons. Lastly, the preacher was 'on full plan' and allowed to preach unaccompanied.

In order to become a Local Preacher in today's Methodist Church a person has to follow a clear process. To become a Methodist Local Preacher, Graham first spoke to his minister and then had an interview with the superintendent who recommended him to the Local Preachers' Meeting. It was the meeting of Local Preachers that approved Graham's appointment as a trainee. At this point Graham was put 'on note' by the Local Preachers' Meeting and was issued with a written note from the superintendent authorizing him to assist a preacher in the conduct of services within the circuit.

During this time a mentor was appointed to help Graham with the practical training and a tutor appointed to oversee the study elements. As part of his training Graham has to assist his mentor with the preparation and leading of services and he also begins to study. Graham initially followed units one to three of the Faith and Worship programme, which include study of the Gospel of Mark and of preaching and worship.

In these first three months, Graham progressed by taking a full service in the presence of two preachers who evaluated the service and reported to the Local Preachers' Meeting. Satisfactory completion of this first part of training moved Graham on to the stage 'on trial', which can last two to five years.

Graham's mentor continued to work with him over the next six months. After that a brief report on a service conducted by Graham was presented to the Local Preachers' Meeting each quarter. At this stage Graham had his first formal interview on the specifics of his Christian experience and on his experience of preaching; he was also asked to explore the challenges that are posed by being 'on trial'.

After this process, as the meeting agreed to allow him to continue 'on trial', Graham moved on to the second part of the course and had to prepare and lead a second trial service in the presence of two preachers, one of whom was a minister. Graham's service was once again reported to the circuit Local Preachers' Meeting. Graham then underwent his second interview in the context of the Local Preachers' Meeting, where he was asked about his faith and his maturing Christian experience. At this stage, Graham also had to know about the Methodist doctrinal standards and to accept and observe the duties of a Local Preacher. Only after this process could Graham be admitted as a Local Preacher, at a special public service. After a year of accreditation Graham completed a project and made a ten-minute presentation on the project to the Local Preachers' Meeting.

Over the time 'on trial', Graham studied a number of modules on the Bible, the teaching of Jesus, the prophets, the work of the Holy Spirit and on the way of Christ. These modules should have influenced Graham's thinking, and when Graham had satisfied the superintendent minister with an oral examination on religious experience, knowledge of and loyalty to Methodist doctrine in particular, to Christian doctrine in general and his willingness to submit to Methodist discipline, the superintendent minister reported to the circuit meeting. As the candidate's general effectiveness in preaching and in Christian work and his personal character were considered satisfactory, Graham could be received as a fully accredited Local Preacher.

On admission to the office, Graham will be accountable to the Local Preachers' Meeting, whose responsibility it is to oversee all Local Preachers. Each Local Preacher is accountable to the meeting. The Methodist Church believes that an annual consideration of the duties and rights of Local Preachers provides an opportunity to remind the meeting of the need for accountability and review.

In order to act as a Local Preacher, Graham is admitted through the admission service for Local Preachers. This service has developed since 1913, and the admission of Local Preachers' service in the *Methodist Worship Book* (Methodist Church, 1999) now states:

The Church of Christ exists to glorify God the Father, who has revealed the way of salvation in the life, ministry and victory of Christ, and has given the Holy Spirit to inspire Christian proclamation and preaching.

From the early days of Methodism, God has called lay people to lead worship and prayer, and to preach the Gospel. In every generation since, women and men have responded to this call and have been admitted as local preachers.

Local Preachers are called to be worthy in character, to lead God's people in prayer and praise, and to share in the Church's mission in the whole world.

N and N, yours is a responsibility rooted in the word of God. You will bring the message of salvation to all, in season and out of season. As you lead worship, and offer good news to others, your life will be shaped and transformed.

At the service, Graham became an authorized lay preacher and continues to work as a postman and lay preacher. He feels that he is following in the footsteps of loyal and good preachers like Thomas

Maxfield and takes his role seriously. Graham also feels that being a postman and a lay preacher keeps him rooted in life and allows him to reflect more fully on God in the world.

TO DO

- What is your experience of Methodist Local Preachers?
- Explore with your local Methodist church the role of their Local Preacher(s).
- What skills and gifts would seem to be necessary for this ministry?

Conclusion

This chapter has looked at the ministry of Reader in the Church of England and of Local Preacher in the Methodist Church. It has explored the historical development of both ministries and set them in the context of ministry today. The recruitment and training of both these ministries reveals the seriousness with which both denominations support and believe in these ministries.

Further reading

Church of England, 2008, *Reader Upbeat: Quickening the Tempo of Reader Ministry in the Church Today*, General Synod Report GS1689. www.cofe.anglican.org/about/generalsynod/agendas/gs1689.rtf

Kuhrt, G. W. and Nappin, P. (eds), 2002, *Bridging the Gap: Reader Ministry Today*, London: Church House Publishing.

Milburn, G. and Batty, M. (eds), 1995, *Workaday Preachers*, Peterborough: Methodist Publishing House.

Rowling, C. and Gooder, P., 2009, *Reader Ministry Explored*, London: SPCK.

Shier-Jones, A., 2008, *The Making of Ministry*, Peterborough: Epworth Press.

7

Called to Ministry as Priest and Presbyter

Introduction

This chapter begins by listening to how an Anglican priest and a Methodist circuit minister discuss their respective vocations and ministries. These accounts are set in conversation with ways in which the Anglican Church and the Methodist Church test vocations to ordained ministry, offer training and formation for ordained ministry, and deploy those ordained within parish and circuit ministry. Particular attention is given to the rites of ordination used. This chapter is designed to help us assess our own sense of vocation to ordained ministry.

Introducing Jayne and Andrew

Jayne is an Anglican priest serving in a rural area and has responsibility for six churches. Jayne was ordained six years ago and this is the first parish over which she has had sole charge. When Jayne was 18, she was thinking about becoming a teacher, but one Sunday a friend said he thought that Jayne would make a good priest. In that instant, Jayne had the strongest sense that she had ever had that God was calling her to service in the Church. Jayne went to university and trained as a teacher, but all through her training and the first three years of working as a teacher Jayne felt called more and more to ministry in the Church. Jayne's call needed to be tested, however, first with close friends and family and in the local church, and eventually by her diocese and bishop and (later) by a national selection conference. Once selected, Jayne's calling was again tested by her training institution. By the time Jayne was ordained, her sense of calling had grown and been stretched, matured and tested through a number of life experiences and experiences in training. Jayne now recognizes that her sense of call will develop and change as she experiences the many challenges of ministry.

Andrew is a presbyter, a minister of word and sacrament in the Methodist Church. He is stationed in a circuit of nine churches and this is his second stationing. Andrew worked as an electrician before being called, first to train as a Local Preacher and latterly as a minister of word and sacrament. It was Andrew's minister who first suggested to him that he think about becoming a Local Preacher. As Andrew had no formal qualifications this took a number of years; then, after having been a Local Preacher, his minister suggested that he think about ordination. Having gained experience of being a Local Preacher, Andrew candidated for full-time ministry. Andrew's candidating process took a year once he had made an initial enquiry. He trained at an ecumenical theological college before spending two years as a probationer serving in an industrial town. He was ordained at the Methodist Conference and now serves as a minister in a seaside circuit.

Jayne and Andrew were called in different ways to serve the Church. A person's call to follow as Jesus' disciple will be different for everyone. In the Bible we see that when Jesus called Nathaniel he is confident and certain, ready to follow instantly (John 1.43–51). When Jesus calls the Samaritan woman at the well, however, she is hesitant, more conscious of her mistakes in life than of her potential (John 4.7–42). Each person also responds differently to the call.

When testing a call to ordained ministry it is clear that there will be a variety of stories of call. For example, when Jayne spoke initially to her vicar about her call, she was aware that her vicar had responded to the call to ministry later in life and through the death of his wife. When Andrew responded to the call he recognized that the call had come from the Church who recognized his gifts.

> **TO DO**
>
> Do you have a sense of call to ordained ministry?
>
> - If you do, how would you describe your call to ordained ministry to people who don't know you well? Try writing down your Christian journey and the key moments that brought you to this place.
> - If you do not have a sense of God's call to ordained ministry, where do you think God is leading you?

Called to ministry as a priest

Since the professionalization of the clergy for ordained ministry, candidates in the Anglican Church have gone through some form of selection process.

Today the selection of candidates for ordained ministry is a continuous process, which begins as soon as an individual becomes aware of a call and vocation. There is a sense of self-selection at this stage, as the person engages with the expectations and requirements, and as they begin to tell family and friends and their local vicar.

If the vicar feels that the candidate does have a calling, the diocesan director of ordinands (DDO) is informed and the candidate meets with the DDO on a regular basis. Each diocese in the Anglican Church may have its own policy for discerning vocations, but there are broad similarities. As the DDO gets to know the candidate over a number of months and in some cases years, the candidate will be encouraged to provide evidence of a vocation and also of the skills and gifts necessary for ordained ministry. Within the selection process there are certain criteria that need to be met before a candidate can be selected for ordination training. These are set out in the document *Shaping the Future: New Patterns of Training for Lay and Ordained* (Archbishops' Council, 2006).

As the DDO continues to explore with the candidate, it becomes clear to both parties whether the call is authentic. At any point during these explorations the DDO may indicate that he or she is unable to affirm the candidate's vocation any further. Or it may be that candidates themselves come to the conclusion that this is not what God is calling them to.

If the process has developed positively, however, the DDO will ask the candidate to meet the bishop or the bishop's examining chaplain. The next stage of the process, if DDO and bishop or bishop's examining chaplain are in agreement, is for the person to attend a selection conference. Some dioceses send candidates directly to the national selection conference, while other dioceses have a two-stage approach and send candidates to a diocesan selection panel before sending them to the national selection conference. At a selection conference candidates are observed over a number of days, undergo a number of formal interviews with selectors and engage with a range of exercises alongside other candidates.

Throughout the process, those who have responsibility to discern and select will be guided by the selection criteria as stated in *Shaping the Future*. These selection criteria are grouped under nine headings:

- Vocation
- Ministry within the Church of England (or Church in Wales, or whatever Anglican Church the candidate is seeking to serve in)
- Spirituality
- Personality and character
- Relationships
- Leadership and collaboration
- Mission and evangelism
- Faith
- Quality of mind

Within each heading, searching questions will be asked about the candidate's sense of vocation and their understanding of the Church into which they are being called. The candidates may be asked about their daily pattern of prayer or their understanding of priesthood. They will be asked how they relate to others and about their leadership style. They will also be observed to see if what they say matches what they do in practice. (For further information, see www.churchofengland.org/clergy-office-holders.)

Jayne remembers her selection conference well and the searching questions that were asked of her. She remembers being asked about the books she had read and which ones excited her and which ones challenged her. She also remembers the group exercises that enabled the selectors to observe her leadership style. The most difficult part of the whole process for Jayne was trying to articulate what vocation was and how her sense of vocation had changed as she grew in faith.

After the selection conference the selectors discern each candidate's calling and capabilities and then recommend to the diocesan bishop whether the person should continue to discern the call through theological education. It is important to note two things. First, the selectors recommend to the bishop and the bishop is the person who makes the final decision. Second, at this stage the recommendation is to train for ministry, not to be accepted for ministry. Acceptance for ministry comes later when the outcome of the training process can be assessed.

The outcome of the selection conference and the report will be discussed with each candidate. The DDO will then discuss with the candidate further training needs. In Jayne's case the DDO guided her towards full-time residential training, but there are other ways to train. There is mixed-mode training or training on a local course, which is validated by a university and often part time.

TO DO

What skills and gifts do you think the Anglican Church should seek in candidates for ordination?

How do you think the Church should examine candidates for these qualities?

Called to ministry as a presbyter

The Methodist Church has a similar process for discerning if a person has a call to ordained ministry. Andrew was already a Local Preacher when he was selected for ordained ministry, but he still went through foundation training before going on to be trained full time at Queen's College, Birmingham. The report *Shaping the Future* also gives a set of learning outcomes for those people candidating for ordained ministry. These were also agreed by the Methodist Conference. The learning outcomes suggest a number of criteria and competences necessary for the candidate at the point of entry into foundation training, at the end of foundation training, at the point of stationing and at ordination. As Andrew went through the candidating procedure at circuit, district and connexional level he was assessed on these learning outcomes.

The new process of candidating for the Methodist Church is set out in a document called *Steps in Candidating for Ordained Ministry in the Methodist Church* (Methodist Church, 2012). The process of candidating begins in September when the candidate completes an online enquiry form; this is followed by the completion of an application form. Reports are written as part of this process and the candidate has to produce a portfolio. This portfolio is a collection of evidence designed to demonstrate a candidate's: personal journey to discernment; understanding of their call; participation in, and understanding of, the Methodist Church; understanding of leadership; engagement with learning (the C2 Candidating Portfolio, 2014, Methodist Church, www.methodist.org.uk).

Then the formal process begins in mid-December. There are three stages to the process. First, the candidate is presented to the circuit meeting, which is followed by the candidate appearing before the district candidate committee. At this stage the candidate has interviews and does a creative presentation. The next stage is to attend a 24-hour connexional committee, known as the candidates selection committee. During this period of time the candidate undergoes formal interviews and group work. The final stage of the process is the agreement of Methodist Conference. (For more information on this process, see www.methodist.org.uk/candidates.)

In terms of what the Methodist Church is looking for in a candidate, the booklet *Is God Calling You?* (Methodist Church, 2010) sets out the criteria and process of selection. The document suggests that the Methodist Church is looking for people who can relate to others, engage in God's world, reach further than the church community, show leadership potential and are both eager to learn and able to communicate.

TO DO

What skills and gifts do you think the Methodist Church should seek in candidates for ordination?

How do you think the Church should examine candidates for these qualities?

What skills and gifts do you think God has given *you* to serve God as an ordained person?

What further skills do you think you need in order to serve in the Church?

Training for ordained ministry

When both processes are complete, a recommendation is given to train for the Anglican Church or Methodist Church. Whatever the mode of training, those preparing for ministry need to be aware that formation and training involves 'knowing God better; knowing yourself better and being changed; understanding and serving the church; understanding and caring for God's world' (Croft and Walton, 2008, p. 13). This summary of training applies both to Methodists and Anglicans in training. As already indicated, this understanding of training is further worked out in a set of learning outcomes found in the report *Shaping the Future*.

For Jayne and Andrew there was the daily routine at theological college of worship that helped them to know God better. Worship and prayer was a community activity, and Jayne and Andrew found that worshipping alongside people from different traditions and in different styles helped them to appreciate the different ways that people come to know God.

Jayne's and Andrew's own personal prayer life grew as they talked through with their spiritual director or soul friend their relationship with God and how training was changing that relationship.

Jayne and Andrew also found that their knowledge of God grew as they studied the Bible. Both were used to Bible study, but had never studied either the Old Testament or New Testament in great detail. They learned how to compare texts from the Bible, about history in the Bible and how to interpret the word for preaching.

TO DO

Write down some of the things you are sure of about God.

- How did you come to know them?
- How did you come to know God?
- How can people get to know God better?

Alongside their study of the Bible, Jayne and Andrew learned how to plan and lead worship. They explored different forms of spirituality, they developed different styles of worship and learned about the sacraments of the Church.

Jayne and Andrew also looked at the Christian tradition. They learned about the doctrines of the Church, including the great creeds. They studied church history and the ways in which Christians have separated from one another because of their different understandings of Christian truth. They studied the foundation documents of their own Churches, including the Book of Common Prayer and the sermons and letters of John Wesley.

A major part of training is looking at yourself and understanding yourself. Both Jayne and Andrew found that in training for ministry they needed to pay great attention to who they are, their integrity of life, their maturity (both strengths and weaknesses), their gifts, their lifestyle and the ways in which they relate to others. At the heart of the Christian understanding of any kind of ministry lies the person's personality and character. Who a person *is* is as important, if not more important, than what a person knows or what a person can do. Ministry is about people, and to understand people ministers need to understand themselves.

TO DO

How would you describe yourself to someone you have never met?

Make a list of what you think are your best qualities?

Think of an experience that helped you learn about yourself.

During both Jayne's and Andrew's training, their formation was important. Formation places the emphasis on personal growth and change, alongside learning new knowledge and skills. An important part of all formation for ministry is deepening and extending an understanding and experience of the life of the Church. This is undertaken through practical placements in a range of different situations. There are also courses designed to help gain an understanding of the Church, which include evangelism, nurture and Christian education, preaching, pastoral care, congregational studies and looking at the roots of the Anglican and Methodist traditions and at the ecumenical movement.

Finally, there is the need to understand God's world, and Jayne and Andrew were introduced to the insights of sociology and psychology in order to reflect on the complex culture of the twenty-first century in which there is a great diversity of basic values and patterns of thinking, often very different from our own.

Having completed training, Jayne was ordained as a deacon for a year before being ordained as a priest. To understand the role of deacon and priest in the Anglican Church, reference needs to be made to the Ordinal. In the ordination service for deacons, the Ordinal says:

> Deacons are called to work with the Bishop and the priests with whom they serve as heralds of Christ's kingdom. They are to proclaim the gospel in word and deed, as agents of God's purposes of love. They are to serve the community in which they are set, bringing to the Church the needs and hopes of all the people. They are to work with their fellow members in searching out the poor and weak, the sick and lonely and those who are oppressed and powerless, reaching into the forgotten corners of the world, that the love of God may be made visible.
>
> Deacons share in the pastoral ministry of the Church and in leading God's people in worship. They preach the word and bring the needs of the world before the Church in intercession. They accompany those searching for faith and bring them to baptism. They assist in administering the sacraments; they distribute communion and minister to the sick and housebound.
>
> Deacons are to seek nourishment from the Scriptures; they are to study them with God's people, that the whole Church may be equipped to live out the gospel in the world. They are to be faithful in prayer, expectant and watchful for the signs of God's presence, as he reveals his kingdom among us. (Church of England, 2007b)

In her year as a deacon, Jayne shared in the ministry of a city-centre parish with her training incumbent. Her training continued as she learned how to serve the community, the people and the Church. She spent time getting to know the people and the community. She learned how to lead worship, administer the sacraments and preach the word of God. As Rosalind Brown (2005, p. 3) wrote in her book *Being a Deacon Today*, 'Deacons are rooted in the local church, living out with the people there – whether regular worshippers or not – a life that reflects the love of Christ.' For Jayne in that first year that was how she understood her ministry as a deacon.

After a year as a deacon, Jayne was ordained as priest. In the ordination service for priests in *Common Worship*, the Ordinal says:

Priests are called to be servants and shepherds among the people to whom they are sent. With their Bishop and fellow ministers, they are to proclaim the word of the Lord and to watch for the signs of God's new creation. They are to be messengers, watchmen and stewards of the Lord; they are to teach and to admonish, to feed and provide for his family, to search for his children in the wilderness of this world's temptations, and to guide them through its confusions, that they may be saved through Christ forever. Formed by the word, they are to call their hearers to repentance and to declare in Christ's name the absolution and forgiveness of their sins.

With all God's people, they are to tell the story of God's love. They are to baptize new disciples in the name of the Father, and of the Son, and of the Holy Spirit, and to walk with them in the way of Christ, nurturing them in the faith. They are to unfold the Scriptures, to preach the word in season and out of season, and to declare the mighty acts of God. They are to preside at the Lord's table and lead his people in worship, offering with them a spiritual sacrifice of praise and thanksgiving. They are to bless the people in God's name. They are to resist evil, support the weak, defend the poor, and intercede for all in need. They are to minister to the sick and prepare the dying for their death. Guided by the Spirit, they are to discern and foster the gifts of all God's people, that the whole Church may be built up in unity and faith. (Church of England, 2007b)

Since her ordination as priest, Jayne has worked alongside her training incumbent and more recently alongside a self-supporting minister, a Reader and various worship leaders. She sees herself working alongside and with people both inside and outside the Church. She sees her main role as teaching and preaching the gospel both in word and deed. She feels called, as David Heywood suggests, to 'animate the church not simply by calling out, equipping and directing its shared ministry, but by helping the church to recognise and grow into its true shape as the beloved, chosen and Spirit-filled servant of the Lord' (2011, p. 197).

After college, Andrew began his probation period for two years and after that period was ordained at the Methodist Conference. At the ordination service, the following charge was addressed to the candidates:

In his name you are
to preach by word and deed the Gospel of God's grace;
to declare God's forgiveness of sins to all who are penitent;
to baptize, to confirm
and to preside at the celebration of the sacrament of Christ's
   body and blood;
to lead God's people in worship, prayer and service;
to minister Christ's love and compassion;
to serve others in whom you serve the Lord himself.
These things are your common duty and delight. In them you
   are to watch over one another in love.
In all things, give counsel and encouragement to those whom
   Christ entrusts to your care.
Pray without ceasing.
Work with joy in the Lord's service.
Let no one suffer hurt through your neglect.
(Methodist Church, 1999)

Andrew's ministry as presbyter can, therefore, be summarized and characterized under three headings. It is a ministry of *word*, which includes (formal and informal) preaching, evangelism, apologetics, theological and prophetic interpretation, teaching and the articulation of faith and human experience. It is a ministry of *sacrament*, which includes presiding at acts of celebration and devotion, especially baptism (and, in the wider sense of sacramental acts, confirmation) and Eucharist. It is a ministry of *pastoral responsibility*, which includes oversight, direction, discipline, order and pastoral care.

Reflecting on his ministry, Andrew can check how well he fulfils the tasks of a presbyter listed in the 2002 Methodist Conference report, *What is a Presbyter?* (Methodist Church, 2002). According to the report a presbyter is someone who:

- prays personally, publicly, and representatively;
- studies the Bible intelligently and interprets the Bible for the local community;
- is actively involved in planning, leading and participating in acts of worship and in acts of mission;
- presides at Holy Communion, Baptism, and Confirmation;
- shares in pastoral responsibility with other presbyters, usually exercising oversight in Christian communities;
- is responsible for the pastoral care of church members, working in collaboration with appropriate church bodies, lay officers and ordained colleagues;
- represents the Church in the community;
- seeks to grow as a woman or man of God and enables others to grow in their discipleship;
- ensures that his or her family and personal commitments are not neglected.

TO DO

Read the ordination services in *The Methodist Worship Book*, beginning on page 297, or in the Anglican Ordinal of the Church of England (in www.churchofengland.org/prayer-worship/worship/texts/ordinal.aspx).

As you read, where do you 'see' yourself? Jot down some notes of your thoughts and feelings about the role of the ordained person.

Conclusion

This chapter has explored the call to ordained ministry in the Anglican and the Methodist Churches. It has concentrated on the call to ministry as a priest in the Anglican Church and the call to ministry as a presbyter in the Methodist Church. The chapter began by exploring the vocational route from call into the discernment process and selection process in both Churches. Then the chapter looked at the training for ordained ministry on a full-time residential basis through to ordination in these Churches.

Further reading

Brown, R., 2005, *Being a Deacon Today: Exploring a Distinctive Ministry in the Church and the World*, Norwich: Canterbury Press.

Croft, S., 2008, *Ministry in Three Dimensions*, new edn, London: Darton, Longman & Todd.

Croft, S. and Walton, R., 2008, *Learning for Ministry: Making the Most of Study and Training*, London: Church House Publishing.

Heywood, D., 2011, *Reimagining Ministry*, London: SCM Press.

Luscombe, P. and Shreeve, E. (eds), 2006, *What is a Minister?*, Peterborough: Epworth Press.

Shier-Jones, A., 2008, *The Making of Ministry*, Peterborough: Epworth Press.

8

Called to Ordained Local Ministry, Pioneer Ministry and the Ministry of Deacon

Introduction

This chapter begins by listening to the experiences of ordinary Christians about the range of ordained ministries across different denominations. These accounts are then set in conversation with the historic understandings of authorized ministries in different denominations. Particular attention is given to ministry leadership in the Anglican and Methodist Churches, especially through the ordained local minister, the pioneer minister and the ministry of deacons. This chapter is designed to help us to assess our own sense of call and vocation to ministries in today's Church.

Introducing Rachel, Rhys, Lynne and Matt

Rachel is an ordained local minister in the Anglican Church. She was called out from her parish after it had developed a lay ministry team and a collaborative approach to ministry. Rachel works locally and her family have lived in the area for generations. Rachel's calling to ordained ministry came late in life; she is now 50. When her parish suggested her as a person for ordained ministry, Rachel struggled to reconcile the call of the Church with her own personal calling. After a period of reflection, Rachel agreed to test the call. She was selected for training and trained alongside the lay people in her local church. Since ordination, Rachel has continued to work closely with the local ministry team and feels called to minister in her local church. She does not feel that she is called to work in other churches in other parts of the country.

Rhys is a deacon in the Methodist Church. Rhys had to candidate and train to be a deacon. He works now as a university chaplain at a busy university campus. The main part of his job is to be present at the university during the week and at worship with the students on Sunday at the local Methodist church. He very much sees his ministry as a servant ministry, modelling Christ's self-emptying and self-offering love. Rhys sees himself as a person who directs himself to political, social and environmental action. He sees his ministry as crossing boundaries, making connections between the Church, the world and the students to whom he ministers.

Lynne is a deacon in the Anglican Church. She has been ordained for six years and works in a parish with five churches. Lynne serves mainly in the church on a local housing estate that has a high rate of both unemployment and teenage pregnancies. Lynne felt called to the diaconate some 20 years ago, but struggled with ordination to the priestly ministry. When her vicar said that he thought she would make a good deacon because of her voluntary work on the estate, Lynne confessed to him her sense of call. Lynne then began the journey to ordination. She was interviewed by the diocesan director of ordinands (DDO) and the bishop and was selected by the same national selection conference as potential priests. Since ordination, Lynne has continued to serve as deacon in the same parish. In this parish there is a team ministry, and Lynne works collaboratively alongside priests, Readers and other lay people. She helps to facilitate the whole Church to live out its baptismal call to serve as Christ in the world, discerning the key issues of injustice and need and developing effective strategies to 'make a difference'. For Lynne, the diaconate represents and has as its focus 'Christ the servant', and she feels called to remind the Church of its diaconal responsibilities and to challenge the world beyond the Church to tackle injustice and need.

Matt is a pioneer minister in the centre of a busy city. The church of which he is a part is developing ministry to young people. Before being ordained, Matt worked as a chaplaincy assistant at the local college of further education and has felt called to work with young people for a number of years. Matt saw his chaplain at college and spoke about his call to pioneer ministry. After some reflection, Matt put himself forward for selection for this ministry. The process of selection was slightly different to the way the chaplain was selected, but Matt enjoyed the experience and then spent two years training for ministry. He is now enjoying finding new ways of working with young people and new ways of being church. Matt is excited about the fresh expressions movement (see www.freshexpressions. org.uk).

Ordained local ministry in the Church of England

During the second half of the twentieth century, the Church of England began seriously to re-examine the long-established separation between holy orders and secular work and to develop new forms of ordained ministry that involved the integration of ordination with secular employment. In so doing, the ground was prepared for ministry in secular employment (MSE) and non-stipendiary ministry (NSM). More recently, non-stipendiary ministry has been restyled self-supporting ministry (SSM).

From 1972 various dioceses experimented with the idea of ordained local ministry. One of the first documented experiments in ordained local ministry was initiated in Bethnal Green under the direction of Ted Roberts. By 2003 there were 19 OLM schemes authorized by the House of Bishops and 217 candidates in training (Bowden, Francis, Jordan and Simon, 2011).

The OLM schemes were originally diocesan initiatives, but the Church of England was keen to watch, monitor and regulate these local developments. Accordingly, the Advisory Council for the Church's Ministry (Church of England, 1987) published the first *Regulations for Non-Stipendiary Ministry* as approved by the House of Bishops in February 1987. Almost immediately after this initial publication a working party was established to review these regulations. The recommendations and regulations proposed by this working party were agreed by the House of Bishops, subject to some amendments, in January 1991 and published by the Advisory Board of Ministry as *Local NSM* (Church of England, 1991a). Core to the recommendations was the following statement:

> Local Non-Stipendiary Ministry is part of the ministry of Christ which he shares with all baptised members of the church. Those called to this ministry by their local church need to have made the calling their own. For its effective operation, LNSM requires the local church's commitment to shared ministry, including the collaboration of local church leaders, ordained and lay. It is a development in ministry open to parishes and candidates of all social backgrounds. (p. ii)

It is to this 1991 report that all other reports refer and on which they build. In that report, ordained local ministry (OLM) is referred to as local non-stipendiary ministry (LNSM) and the following definition is given: 'LNSM is a form of ordained ministry whereby men and women are called out by a local church for ministry within a specific locality' (p. 1).

The report gives five motives for LNSM: a renewed appreciation of the significance of variety of ministries, the importance of the local, the wish to encourage indigenous ministries, the value of collaborative ministry, and the recognition that a shortage of stipendiary clergy will emerge. The 1991 report also suggests the following necessary marks of OLM: Catholic order in the service of the local church and community, the collaborative ministry of the whole local church, and a commitment to working in teams. It goes on to stress that an OLM scheme must have a full place in the life of the diocese.

Rachel feels that her ministry is among the baptized of her local church. She enjoys sharing ministry with other lay people who have responsibility for worship, pastoral visiting and mission in the parish. Before ordination Rachel was part of the ministry team and her responsibility was preparing and leading informal worship as an authorized worship leader. Her family were farmers and Rachel never felt she would be able to follow a ministry training course, but with the help of her fellow lay ministers she grew in knowledge and understanding.

Rachel may never have considered ordination if it had not been the local church who called her into ministry in her own locality. Rachel's ministry is local to where she was born and brought up. Rachel is serving in the church in which she was baptized as a baby, but she recognizes that she is part of a bigger Church and is committed to being a part of the deanery and diocese. She knows that she is part of the Holy Catholic Church and has always supported the work of her bishop and diocese.

TO DO

Have you had experience of people who are ordained to local ministry?

What do you think are the strengths of ordained local ministry?

What do you think are the difficulties with ordained local ministry?

Deacons in the Methodist Church

The origins of the Methodist Diaconal Order in Britain lie in the foundation of the Wesley Deaconess Order. In 1890 Revd Thomas Bowman Stephenson developed the order to meet the physical, social and spiritual needs of those living in deprived inner-city areas and disadvantaged rural communities (Jackson, 2008). The Wesley Deaconess Order, as it became known, ended in 1979. In 1986, however, the British Methodist Conference called for the order to be reopened. This call came as a result of the debate on a Methodist

Conference report entitled *The Ministry of the People of God* (Methodist Church, 2000). In 1998, after a period of reflection on the nature of the diaconal ministry, the Methodist Conference determined that the Methodist Diaconal Order was to be regarded as an order of ministry as well as a religious order. The most recent statement on the nature of the order, *What is a Deacon?*, was approved by the Methodist Conference in 2004.

The Methodist diaconate in Britain differs from that within Roman Catholic, Orthodox and Anglican Churches in that it is not a transitional stage en route to ordination as a priest. Nor, as in many Lutheran Churches, is the Methodist deacon seen as an assistant parochial minister or as exercising a professional ministry in fields such as health, welfare or education. The Methodist diaconate is not a lay office, as is the case in the Reformed and Baptist traditions.

What makes the character of the Methodist Diaconal Order unique is that it seeks to focus for the whole Church what it means to exercise a servant ministry. The Report *What is a Deacon?* states:

Thus, servant ministry is the task and calling of the whole people of God as they seek to continue the work of Christ in the power of the Holy Spirit; taking Christ as pattern and inspiration: 'I am among you as one who serves' (Luke 22.27).

The task of the deacon is to focus that servant ministry in particular. The role of the deacon is to offer a visible expression that
(a) focuses on (draws attention to and makes clear) the nature and meaning of this ministry
(b) encourages and enables others to undertake this ministry with greater effectiveness in their own daily lives

The deacon's primary purpose is to enable others. Deacons also act as a model and sometimes pioneer too. They often possess specialist skills in some aspect of diaconal work yet always work collaboratively, helping others develop their gifts. It is in this sense that the deacon represents, rather than replaces. They are authorised by Conference to be public people representing God-in-Christ to the World and representing the World and Church before God. They constantly seek to serve the needs of the Kingdom in the power of the Spirit through who they are and what they do. (Methodist Church, 2004, p. 3)

Rhys certainly tries to do this in his ministry among students. He tries to enable young students to develop the skills and gifts God has given them. He encourages them to bear witness to Christ in their daily lives. He does this through Bible study and prayer, and Rhys teaches the students to reflect on their own experience in the light of what they have learned, both at university and through reflecting on the word of God.

Building and encouraging community is central to the ministry of the deacon. Rhys in his ministry tries to build community with young people who are away from home for the first time. He tries to build support networks among the students.

Methodist deacons also share a public commitment to follow a rule of life. The deacons' rule of life, set out in the report *What is a Deacon?*, involves a devotional life of collective worship and private daily study and prayer, including a time of intercession for sisters and brothers in the order, regular times of self-examination, use of a spiritual director/companion, making time for retreats or quiet days and meeting with other deacons for study, reflection and worship.

The deacons' rule of life emphasizes a disciplined life with order and rhythm that allows time for study and relaxation, personal relationships, relating to one's local community, mutual practical and prayerful support of fellow deacons, regularly meeting in local groups and annually as a whole order in convocation and also expressing a careful stewardship of time, talents, money and possessions that enjoys and uses God's gifts wisely (Methodist Church, 2004, pp. 12–13).

Rhys regularly prays for his fellow deacons and keeps in touch with them by card, email or phone. He joins regularly in local groups for fellowship and for sharing of insights, resources, joys and sorrows. Rhys also attends the annual national conference for deacons.

TO DO

Reflecting on your experience of deacons in the Methodist Church:

- What are the strengths of the ministry of deacon in the Methodist Church?
- How important is it for everyone to have a rule of life in Christian discipleship and ministry?

The deacon in the Anglican Church

Within the Anglican Church there are three orders of ordained ministry: deacons, priests and bishops. For many people seeking ordination to the priesthood, time spent as a deacon is seen as a transitional stage, usually a year long. For others, the role and work of a deacon is seen as an important ministry within the Anglican Church (Brown, 2005). In fact, the distinctive diaconate is seen as a biblical order of ministry reaching back to the early Church and as such has its own characteristics and responsibilities. These responsibilities, given with the Church's authority, can differ from parish to parish and from town ministry to rural ministry, where clergy resources are often stretched.

The report of the Church of England's Faith and Order Advisory Group, *The Mission and Ministry of the Whole Church* (Church of England, 2007a), building on a previous Church of England report, *For Such a Time as This* (Church of England, 2001), has this to say about the work and role of a deacon:

> The first thing to say about deacons, in the light of the pivotal use of the terms *diakonia* and *diakonos* in the New Testament, especially by St Paul, is that deacons, in their ordination, receive the fundamental commissioning of Christ to be ministers (*diakonoi*) of the gospel. St Ignatius of Antioch calls them 'deacons of the mysteries of Jesus Christ' (cf. 1 Corinthians 4.1). They are sent by

Christ, through the Church, as bearers of the Good News to the world and in this role (as the classic Anglican Ordinal of 1550/1662 particularly emphasizes) they have a special compassionate care for the needs of the sick, the lonely and the oppressed. Together with all Christians and all ministers, theirs is a life of compassionate service in obedience to Christ's command and example – service primarily of Christ and under his authority, secondarily of those who are Christ's and to whom he imparts his authority.

Deacons, like priests and bishops – and lay ministers too, for that matter – are related to the word, the sacraments and pastoral care: they receive the full ministry of the gospel. But they have an assisting, not a presiding role in relation to these three central tasks of the Church's mission. Deacons assist the priest and the bishop and carry out the duties deputed to them in relation to this mandate. They preach, teach and give instruction in the faith. They lead the people in worship and assist in the celebration of the sacraments by bringing candidates, whom they have sought out and prepared, to baptism and (as the 1550/1662 Ordinal says), baptising them in the absence of the priest, and by assisting the president in the Eucharistic liturgy and leading the people in their participation.

Deacons are ministers of pastoral care on behalf of bishop and priest; they carry Christ's compassion to the forgotten corners of society and ensure that the needy receive practical help. Through their role in the liturgy, deacons bring the concerns and petitions of the wider community, within which they minister day by day, to the heart of the Church's worship, in order that these concerns may be laid upon the altar and placed at the foot of the cross (*Common Worship* spells out the role that it is appropriate for deacons to take at the Eucharist). Deacons can cross boundaries, from a parish base, into the 'fresh expressions' dimension of the mixed economy Church. Deacons thus share in the apostolic ministry, being sent by Christ, through the Church as missionaries to carry forward his saving work. (Church of England, 2007a, pp. 77–8)

As a deacon, Lynne sees herself as called to work with the bishop and alongside the priest. Her role, she feels, is to proclaim the gospel – the good news of Christ in her life and work, so that God's love for everyone is seen through her. Lynne seeks inspiration and sustenance from the Scriptures; she tries to model her life upon them and reflects on them together with God's people. Lynne feels that she acts as a bridge between the people and her local church, and she tries to be a constant encouragement to all those whom she serves.

For her selection for training, Lynne went to a three-day selection conference after having interviews with DDO, bishop and diocesan selection panel. The same criteria for selection for ordained ministry were used as those proposed in the document *Shaping the Future* (Archbishops' Council, 2006). However, there were particular aspects of the criteria that were accentuated for a vocation to the diaconate. The additional points to consider in assessing a candidate for the diaconate are taken from the report *The Distinctive Diaconate* (Diocese of Salisbury, 2003) and include some of the following issues under the regular nine headings.

Under the first heading of *vocation*, the criteria are looking for a strong sense of vocation to the ministry of the deacon, not a failed or thwarted sense of vocation to priesthood. There has to be a sense of a life-calling from God, not a potentially passing desire to engage in the Church's ministry.

Under the second heading of *ministry within the Church of England*, the criteria are looking for engagement with a servant ministry, a responsible behind-the-scenes person, able to get on with things out of the limelight and to oil the wheels for the benefit of others. The deacon is called to be comfortable occupying space on the boundaries, a liminal person who is at ease alongside people on the edges of the Church and society, yet who is also secure and centred within themselves.

Under the third heading of *spirituality*, the criteria are looking for a liturgical sensitivity and presence that enables others to worship, brings the needs of the world into worship and interprets them for the Christian community. This requires a rooted Christian spirituality, grounded in a life of prayer and immersion in God's word, attentive to God's presence in the world.

Under the fourth heading of *personality and character*, the criteria are looking for an attitude that reflects a vocation to be a servant without being a doormat. Such an attitude is reflected in an ability to listen and in extending a welcome to others while respecting their space.

Under the fifth heading of *relationships*, the criteria are looking for an ability to relate to people of different ages and from different social backgrounds. The deacon needs an instinctive ability to get alongside people and to speak their language. The deacon is called to display pastoral skills that care for others appropriately.

Under the sixth heading of *leadership and collaboration*, the criteria are looking for the ability and willingness to work in a team. The deacon is called to be a leader who assists rather than always takes the lead, and does not unsettle or unseat others who have either long-term or short-term responsibilities. The deacon is called to be a public representative person for the Church, one who is competent and comfortable in the public eye, whether in liturgy or the life of the world.

Under the seventh heading of *faith*, the criteria look for a practical faith. The deacon is called to preach the gospel in actions as well as words. The deacon is called to teach by example as well as by instruction.

Under the eighth heading of *mission and evangelism*, the criteria are looking for evidence of engagement with and in the local community, and awareness of what is happening in the wider world. A deacon is called to a life of service within and outside the Christian community.

Under the ninth heading of *quality of mind*, the criteria are looking for an approach that reflects a thirst to know more of God and an ability to interpret what is known for others. The deacon is called to combine creativity and imagination coupled with stability and common sense.

When Lynne went through the selection process, she had to talk to each of the above points in order to assess her calling to the ministry of deacon within the Anglican Church. Her work as a pharmacist in the local hospital enables her to bridge the gap of world and Church in a discreet and unobtrusive way.

The Diocese of Salisbury appears to have undertaken to explore thoroughly the role of deacon through the chairwomanship of Rosalind Brown and the production of the report *The Distinctive Diaconate* (2003). Brown has since developed this work and in 2005 published a book called *Being a Deacon Today: Exploring a Distinctive Ministry in the Church and the World.*

Ordained pioneer ministry

In February 2004, the General Synod of the Church of England welcomed and commended the report, *Mission-Shaped Church: Church Planting and Fresh Expressions of Church in a Changing Context* (Archbishops' Council, 2004). Recommendations 10–15 make reference to ministry training. Of particular significance is the following statement:

> Priority attention needs to be given by the Church of England to the identification and training of leaders for pioneering missionary projects. The possibility of a call to such work needs to be specifically identified in the vocational process … A course, college or other institution with specialist training skills should be identified within each region, to provide key training modules. Similarly, training curacies and similar key first posts should be provided with proven leaders of church plants and fresh expressions of Church. (Church of England, 2004, p. 134)

Since that report, the ministry of ordained pioneer ministers (OPM) has grown and in the early years selection of OPM was exactly the same as candidates for ordained ministry. In March 2010, however, the Ministry Council of the Church of England agreed to separate the discernment for ordained ministry, undertaken at Bishop's Advisory Panels, from the discernment for pioneering ministry. The discernment process for pioneering ministry would now take place at a newly set up Pioneer Panel.

Matt remembers the process of gathering together a portfolio of evidence of his capacity for pioneering work, so that the DDO could send the information to this panel. After completing it he was invited to three one-to-one interviews: a vocational interview, a pastoral interview and an educational interview, each lasting about 90 minutes. After the interviews Matt had to wait for the panel to meet together with the director of fresh expressions to discern his potential. Once the decision was reached, the panel wrote to Matt's sponsoring bishop who then informed Matt. Matt went at a later date to the Bishop's Advisory Panel.

New criteria were also agreed in March 2010. These criteria continue to use the same nine headings used for selection to the priesthood or diaconate: vocation, ministry within the Church of England, spirituality, personality and character, relationships, leadership and collaboration, faith, mission and evangelism, and quality of mind. Three further criteria were also added:

- to show how they have responded to God's call to be pioneering;
- to understand contemporary cultures and the practice of planting fresh expressions of Church within them; and
- to develop a vision for fresh expressions of church in a local context.
  (For further information see: www.churchofengland.org/documentlibrary.aspx?tag=Pioneer%20Ministry)

Matt was selected for training and then went to theological college where he studied for ordained pioneer ministry. Among the work he undertook was a pioneer ministry module, which Matt studied for two terms. Its content included a focus on contemporary culture, mission and evangelism, leadership, character, team-building, entrepreneurship, innovation, sacramental ministry in fresh expressions, planning, starting and leading a fresh expression, identifying and mentoring leaders and evaluating the impact of fresh expressions of church.

Matt also undertook a mission module, which also ran over two terms. This module included teaching and reflection on cross-cultural evangelism, church-planting and fresh expressions of church. The module also included participation in an urban micro-mission and a faith-sharing weekend, undertaken in collaboration with local churches. Other parts to the training also helped Matt to feel confident about his ministry as a pioneer minister.

Matt feels that God is calling him to develop his ministry and to work among young people. He also feels that God is calling him to encourage others to become disciples of Christ.

TO DO

Reflecting on your experience of pioneer ministers in the Church, what are the strengths of pioneer ministers and what are their weaknesses?

Conclusion

This chapter has explored ordained local ministry in the Anglican Church, the ministry of deacon in the Methodist and Anglican Churches and pioneer ministry in the Anglican Church. It has looked at the historical and theological developments of these different ministries and the call to these ministries.

Further reading

Brown, R., 2005, *Being a Deacon Today: Exploring a Distinctive Ministry in the Church and the World*, Norwich: Canterbury Press.

Cray, G., 2004, *Mission-Shaped Church*, London: Church House Publishing.

Jackson, S., 2008, 'The Methodist Diaconal Order: A Sign of the Diaconal Church', in D. Clark (ed.), *The Diaconal Church*, Peterborough: Epworth Press, pp. 159–70.

Kuhrt, G. W. and Nappin, P. (eds), 2002, *Bridging the Gap: Reader Ministry Today*, London: Church House Publishing.

Shier-Jones, A., 2009, *Pioneer Ministry and Fresh Expression of Church*, London: SPCK.

9

Called to Self-Supporting Ministry and Ordained Ministry in Secular Employment

Introduction

This chapter begins by listening to how two Anglican priests and one Methodist presbyter describe their vocations and ministries outside the conventional structures. Owen is a manager of a supermarket and serves as a minister in secular employment (MSE). His job means that he is expected to work on Sundays and has no fixed duties in a parish. Jean is a retired teacher and serves as a self-supporting priest (SSM), living in a rural rectory. Ian is a doctor in a hospital; he serves as a sector minister in the hospital and is stationed in his local circuit. These accounts are set in conversation with current thinking in the Church on these diverse expressions of ordained ministry. The chapter is designed to help us assess our own sense of vocation to ordained ministry.

Introducing Owen, Jean and Ian

Owen works in a national supermarket chain as one of its local managers and serves as a minister in secular employment (MSE). His job means that he is expected to work on Sundays and he has no fixed duties in a parish. For Owen, being a priest in the workplace is very important and the connection between prayer, the sacraments and his work is central to his understanding of his call to ministry. Owen feels called to minister where he works and over the years he has built up good relationships with his colleagues, which allows him to minister to them in both the joys and sorrows of life.

Jean is a retired teacher and serves as a self-supporting priest (SSM). Now that she is retired, Jean lives in a rural rectory with her husband Michael and serves there without drawing a stipend. Her ministry is often referred to as 'house for duty'. Jean has now served this parish of four churches for the past three years. Previously, she taught in a school some 30 miles away and was ordained priest while working full time. Jean feels called to work in the parish where she lives and she prefers to focus her ministry in the local church and community.

Ian is a sector minister in a hospital. He works as a doctor and is based in the hospital chaplaincy. Ian lives over 20 miles away from the hospital, is stationed in his local circuit and his preaching appointments are on the local plan. Ian was selected for ministry in the same way as his fellow ministers who are stationed in circuits. It was during his training that a tutor suggested to him that a sector appointment may be more fitting as he could use his skills as a doctor as well as a minister. Ian feels called to minister both in his place of work and also to preach and lead worship in his circuit.

The case for self-supporting clergy

The idea of self-supporting ministry goes back to the time of Paul in the New Testament, who wrote of financing his living expenses as a missionary by continuing his trade as a tent-maker (1 Corinthians 9.14–15). This biblical precedent was developed again at the beginning of the twentieth century. Clergy like Roland Allen campaigned for voluntary clergy because of their value in the mission fields. In his book *Voluntary Clergy* (1923), Allen maintained that people who lived in remote places should receive the sacraments and that not to be given the sacraments was unjustifiable just because there were no professional clergy to take the service.

TO DO

Read 1 Corinthians 9.14–15.

Can you find any other references to the call to ministry and to the experience of supporting those in ministry in the New Testament?

In your reflections, how practical do you think it would be for *all* ministry to be self-supporting?

What are the advantages of ministry in secular employment?

Rediscovery of mixing ministry and work

From the Fourth Ecumenical Council at Chalcedon in the fifth century to the end of the reformations of the sixteenth century, it had been the general practice of the Christian Church in Western Europe to discourage those who have taken up holy orders from participating in secular work (DeLashmutt, 2008). In the English Reformation, clergy were forbidden by the Pluralities Act of 1529 to engage in activities that could be construed as trade or dealing in goods or merchandise (Hacking, 1990). This was further emphasized in the Ordinal of the Church of England's first Prayer Book of 1549. The bishop was to charge his ordinands to set aside worldly cares and apply themselves wholly to ministry.

It took almost 300 years before the Pluralities Act was challenged in 1841 by Thomas Arnold, in a pamphlet arguing for the ordination of working men as deacons. His argument was based on his belief that there would be a shortage of clergy especially in urban areas. The idea lapsed with his death in 1842. Forty-five years later, William Bright, Regius Professor of Ecclesiastical History at Oxford, also pressed for the ordination of working men as deacons. There was, however, a considerable strength of opinion that ordination was a 'profession' and a man could not have two professions (Hacking, 1990).

It was not until 1939 that the Church of England, through its reform of canon law, began to develop non-stipendiary ministry. This committee who were reforming canon law included Mervyn Stockwood, who was to become the bishop responsible for developing training for self-supporting ministers and then ordaining these ministers in his own Diocese of Southwark. The committee looked at 'Of the Manner of Life of Ministers' and outlined three principal reasons for changing the rules relating to the employment of clergy in secular employment.

- The declining numbers of clergy made a supplementary parish ministry essential.
- The men already exercising roles of pastoral responsibility in the secular world would be that much more effective if they were ordained.
- This would be a key way of bridging what was recognized as a gap dividing the life of the Church from the realities of industrial life. (Hacking, 1990, p. 13)

In 1947 the Church of England began the process of amending the canons relating to the life and vocation of priests to include self-supporting ministers. Strict guidelines were drawn up so that priests could work in secular employment following ordination. In 1955 canon law was officially amended to allow for ordained clergy to hold a parochial office while working in secular employment. Finally, the civil law prohibiting clergy from taking up secular employment was revoked in 1964. Since 1964 the Church of England has been attempting to understand this new ministry (Paul, 1964; Advisory Council for the Church's Ministry, 1968; Hodge, 1983; Tiller, 1983; Advisory Board of Ministry, 1998).

In 1963 the first priests were ordained in England as non-stipendiary ministers in secular employment, having trained on the Southwark Ordination Course set up by Bishop Mervyn Stockwood. These pioneers were 'worker priests' (Scott, 2006). At this time there was just one other diocese training people for self-supporting ministry, the Diocese of Gloucester. It was, however, not until 1970 that the bishops' regulations for the selection and training of candidates for auxiliary ministry were provided for guidance for those training for self-supporting ministry. By 1982 there were 15 courses offering training for ordination to the non-stipendiary ministry.

Ministers in secular employment

The difference between a minister in secular employment (MSE) and a self-supporting minister (SSM) can be seen in terms of where ministers place the focus of their ministry. MSEs, like Owen, feel called to exercise their ministry principally through their paid work in the 'secular' world, rather than through the organization of the Church. SSMs, like Jean, see their main focus of active ministry in the church community. Some, like Jean, are retired, while others regard their paid employment as secondary to, or as a means of providing financial support for, their service in the Church.

TO DO

What is your experience of clergy serving in various self-supporting capacities?

What is the difference, in your experience, between the ministry of MSEs and SSMs?

To what kind of ministry are you called?

Through their website the Diocese of Coventry suggests that MSEs feel called to their 'secular' work and have a constructive relationship to it (www.coventry.anglican.org/ministry/ministries/ordained ministry/ministryinsecularemployment). They have a full-time ministry, expressed in full-time work. MSEs are employed exclusively for their role as worker, of whatever kind, and express their priesthood *through* their work as well as 'at work'. Their working life is integral to, and fulfils, their priestly calling. The Diocese of Coventry identifies what it sees to be five characteristics of MSEs.

First, MSEs are called to extend the Church's witness to God's activities beyond the walls of the Church and into the world, especially into the world of work, which has sometimes been undervalued by the Church in its preference for church-based activities. MSEs demonstrate the Church's investment in the workplace.

Second, MSEs are called to extend the awareness of the Church concerning the workplace. They are in the right position to keep the Church better informed about the world of work. As individual ministers, they are also better placed to minister to people in secular employment because of their own experience in different working environments.

Third, like parochial clergy, MSEs are rooted in a community; but while for parochial clergy this tends to be the community where people live, for MSEs it is the community where people work. The important point is that in today's society and for increasing numbers of people it is the workplace more than the local church or the immediate neighbourhood that is the more stable form of community and the source of personal identity.

Fourth, by being embedded in the place of work, MSEs may be well positioned to provide a safe space in which people can seek guidance and explore the issues that are concerning them in their lives. They often enable less conspicuous Christians to declare themselves. The pastoral interactions within the school, hospital or workplace community can be every bit as intense as those in the parish.

Fifth, as accessible priests serving in the workplace, MSEs may be asked to be involved in sacramental ministry as a result of the relationships developed in the workplace. They will, anyway, be involved in the 'secular sacraments' of confession, absolution, healing and blessing.

Mark Hodge and John Mantle give the following summary of self-supporting ministries:

Ministry in secular employment (MSE) may be seen as a 'branch' of non-stipendiary ministry. The majority of NSMs who normally earn their own living and expect to live their faith at work, nevertheless see their ministry as focused *in the life and witness of their parish church.* To this end they assist an incumbent in the administration of word and sacrament, and participate in the teaching and pastoral care of the congregation. In contrast, MSEs, while maintaining a relationship with their parish church and its incumbent, see their ministry focused *in their place of work,* be it school, shop, lab or factory. They enter – in the face of the Church's public faith and public failings – with substantial theological comprehension, pastoral know-how and an authoritative sign and voice *because* they are ordained. (Hodge and Mantle, 2001, pp. 221–2)

Selection and training of self-supporting ministers has over the years raised concerns. The *Bishops' Regulations* (Church of England, 1970) were clear that candidates for non-stipendiary ministry should attend the same conferences as candidates for stipendiary ministry and that the same criteria for selection should apply. This point is also made by the two reports, *A Supporting Ministry* (Advisory Council for the Church's Ministry, 1968) and *Selection for Ministry* (Advisory Council for the Church's Ministry, 1983). Recognizing that the same qualities are needed, *A Supporting Ministry* suggests that there are, however, different criteria that may be required in selecting candidates. It goes on to identify five broad types of non-stipendiary ministry and to argue that each of these categories requires 'subtly different criteria'.

Today MSEs are selected according to the criteria for the selection for ministry in the Church of England, which are applied to all candidates offering themselves for ordained ministry. Owen went to a selection conference with people offering themselves for full-time ministry and he also completed the same application form. While his interviews were conducted under the same broad nine headings as other candidates, there were subtle differences in the criteria.

The Church of England Ministry Division offers distinctive points to DDOs and bishops' advisors when considering the selection of potential MSEs, and these complement the published criteria. Under the same nine headings, according to which candidates for stipendiary ministry, self-supporting ministry and pioneer ministers are selected, the following further criteria are suggested.

Under the first heading of *vocation*, the criteria are looking for a calling that is realistic and informed in relation to workplace ministry *and* ministry within the Church. In other words, the vocation is both to priesthood and to secular work.

Under the second heading of *ministry within the Church of England*, the criteria are looking for integration between the Church of England's understanding of the office and work of deacons and priests and the special context and constraints of the workplace. There are opportunities here to explore how the workplace context may shape the expression of ordained ministry and how the role of MSEs differs from workplace chaplaincies.

Under the third heading of *spirituality*, the criteria are looking for a realistic commitment to a regular devotional life, which draws upon and contributes to the spiritual significance of work and daily life. At the same time, concern is expressed for the person's ability to bring the experience of work into liturgy and preaching.

Under the fourth heading of *personality and character*, the criteria are looking for an ability to be pastorally sensitive and responsive within boundaries set by secular organizations; an ability to define and redefine ministry in changing contexts and a capacity to cope with the stress that arises from the inevitably conflicting demands of family, work and Church.

Under the fifth heading of *relationships*, the criteria are looking for sensitivity and maturity to negotiate and exercise ministry with workplace colleagues, and to communicate effectively with staff at all levels in an organization. This involves an ability to build relation-ships across a wide range of communities.

Under the sixth heading of *leadership and collaboration*, the criteria are looking for an ability to lead from within a team rather than as the team leader. Being sensitive to workplace dynamics, there is also a need for maturity to work within structures while at the same time, where required, challenging their values.

Under the seventh heading of *faith*, the criteria are looking for a grasp of the way in which the Christian faith may be specifically expressed through work. Then, beyond the workplace, there is the need for the ability to make connections between faith and the needs of contemporary society.

Under the eighth heading of *mission and evangelism*, the criteria are looking for an awareness of the issues and problems faced by working communities, as well as organizations and their leaders. Such insights are needed for an authentic and effective workplace minister capable of making connections between faith and working life.

Under the heading of *quality of mind*, the criteria are looking for the capacity to reflect theologically on the demands, needs and privileges of workplace ministry. Such a capacity to reflect theologically resources an ability to respond to the challenges and questions frequently faced by workplace ministers, as visible representatives of the Church of England. MSEs may become a theological resource (for the Church and others) in the workplace. (See www.churchof england.org/media/1324699/ministersinsecularemployment.doc).

Owen remembers the above criteria being used at his selection conference to discern his call to MSE ministry. He found his response to the question about Christian faith and work in particular hard to articulate. After his selection, Owen trained on a local course that enabled him to reflect on his call to be a MSE. Now five years later, he continues to reflect, and in his reflection finds powerful connections between prayer and sacrament and the work he does. He talks about the connection he has both with the people he works with and also with the customers he comes into contact with. He has spent many an hour talking with his work colleagues about the meaning of Christmas and about life and death issues. Owen finds that his work role and context leads naturally to moments requiring confession, absolution, healing and blessing – even though these terms, or any kind of religious language, may never be used. He speaks about how the celebration of the Eucharist reaches out to, informs and incorporates the world of work. Sometimes this is through worship or prayer in or connected with the workplace. However, he is acutely aware of the dangers of 'churchifying' that workplace.

Over the years, Owen has become known at work as the man of faith and finds that his own work colleagues search him out when they need to talk about religious matters. Reflecting on the experience of exercising his workplace ministry, Owen sees how his personal situation maps on to the four characteristics of the ministry of MSEs identified on the Church of England's website. First, it is true that Owen's ministry has a clear *pastoral* element, but one that is defined by 'working alongside' people rather than in a more formally defined chaplaincy role. Second, it is true that Owen's familiarity with the pressures and frustrations of the workplace (as well as with the positive aspects of working life) really shapes his pastoral perspective and that this is appreciated by colleagues. Third, it is true that Owen's ministry has a clear *evangelistic* element, as he connects working experience with gospel values. He has become gifted at bringing the language of faith into the workplace and, indeed, at bringing the language of the workplace into liturgy and worship. Fourth, Owen's ministry has a clear *teaching* element. As part of who he is, as a colleague in the workplace, he finds himself unpacking Christian ideas and Christian values in everyday conversation.

Sector ministry and the Methodist Church

The Methodist Church has a number of forms of ordained ministry. The 1986 report, *The Ministry of the People of God*, gives the following examples:

(a) The itinerant circuit minister who works primarily within, for and from the churches in a circuit.
(b) Some ordained ministers who are called to work primarily at District or Connexional level, in a variety of ways (e.g. President and Secretary of Conference, Divisional Secretaries, College Tutors, District Chairmen).
(c) A few ordained ministers who are seconded to other denominations or ecumenical agencies in ministries whose primary focus is comparable with the range of possibilities covered by (a) and (b).

(d) A considerable number of ministers who pursue their ministry primarily in a secular context, either in a particular institution or in a sector of contemporary secular life. (Methodist Church, 2000, p. 219)

TO DO

What is your experience of Methodist ministers serving in different pastoral contexts?

What is the difference in your experience between those ministers stationed in a particular area with responsibility for a number of churches and those called to serve in the workplace?

Ian is a minister in sector ministry. Sector ministry was introduced in 1968 in the Methodist Church, although for a number of years before 1968 there had been a few ministers each year who were granted 'permission to serve' external organizations like universities and schools. The original explanation for sector ministry in the Methodist Church comes from the report of the Commission on the Church's Ministries in the Modern World (1968). It stated:

In the development of a modern society there is a new and increasing complexity. Most people are now called upon to live in a number of different 'worlds' which are largely independent of each other. They play a different role in each world. They work with a different group in each of these areas. In addition to home and family they include work and industry, social services, education, etc. and it is to these distinct areas which we refer in the use of the word 'sector.' When we talk about the church in a sector we mean the company of Christians there, the community which Christians discover and create within their sector. (Methodist Church, 1968, p. 503)

This category of ministry has changed its name over the years. Before 1969 this type of ministry was understood as 'permission to serve external organizations'. This changed in 1969 to 'sector ministry', and then further renamed ministry in other appointments, with two sub-categories: sector ministries and ordained ministries serving other denominations or ecumenical agencies.

The idea of sector ministry in the Methodist Church has been controversial. For some there was a concern about the whole idea of sector ministry as it was felt that it undermined the unity of Methodist ministry by creating a class of ministers who were not subject to the discipline of the Methodist Conference. There was also the belief that the work of ministers in sector ministry could be done by lay people. While the 1988 Commission on the Ministry of the Whole People of God acknowledged this issue, they also made this point:

> Conference has examined this viewpoint on a number of occasions and each time had reaffirmed its commitment to ministry in the Sectors. Some of the work done by those working in this area is innovative and pioneering; some arises from a deep sense of call and commitment to a particular sector; some is an indication of specific skills which some of our ministers possess or have been encouraged to acquire. Much of it brings new insights and resources into the life of the churches. (Methodist Church, 2000, p. 235)

The Commission recommended a return to the designation 'sector ministry'. The whole debate about sector ministry has continued in the Methodist Church because some continue to challenge its validity. One reason for non-acceptance in the case of some is that there is a single order of presbyters. At the ordination service the President says to the ordinand: 'God has called you into the Order of Presbyters among his people' (Methodist Church, 1999, p. 261). The service does not, however, describe which type of ordained ministry.

In 1975 a report of the Working Group on Sector and Auxiliary Ministers declared that 'ministers are ordained not for the circuit ministry, but for the ministry'. This was further acknowledged in the debate on the report on the Ministry of the Whole People of God: 'There is one ordained ministry. Those who are based in the circuits, together with all other Methodist ministers, participate in it equally, and together constitute its unity' (Methodist Church, 2000, p. 261).

For Clifford Bellamy (2002) the question is not 'is there a theology of sector ministry?' but 'is sector ministry compatible with Methodism's theology of ordained ministry?' Methodist theology of ordination is clear about three aspects. First, the call of God is central, and the Deed of Union and all subsequent reports affirm this. Second, the minister is called to represent and lead all Christian people in their calling and to be an ambassador in the world. Third, the ordained person enables others to fulfil their ministry. Bellamy argues that sector ministry is compatible with Methodism's theology of ordination. He suggests that, while there may be representative and ambassadorial responsibilities within the Church, the ordained minister's representative and ambassadorial responsibilities on behalf of the Church in the world are of equal if not greater importance. The ordained minister is a representative in the Church and the world. Bellamy further argues that the minister in sector ministry is an enabler. He believes that the role of sector ministry does not undermine the work of the laity, but is an aid to the ministry of lay people in the secular world.

Finally, Bellamy argues against those who feel that sector ministry 'disrupts the unity of the Methodist ministry by creating a class of ministers who are not wholly subject to the discipline of the Conference' (2002, p. 55). He believes, rather, that those in sector ministries are in 'full connexion' with the Church. He emphasizes the fact that all sector ministers are stationed in circuits. They are members of the circuit staff, of the circuit meeting and of the church council of every church in the circuit. For Bellamy (2002) and the many reports produced on sector ministry, sector ministry is a valid expression of ordained presbyteral ministry.

> ## TO DO
>
> Do you think that a minister who is ordained to the presbyteral ministry can serve that ministry in different contexts?
>
> What is the difference for you between the different types of ministry in the Methodist understanding of ordination?

Ian sees the focus of his ministry in the workplace and not in the Church. That does not mean that he does not take his turn to preach and lead worship where he is stationed. He does, but he also preaches and leads worship at the hospital chapel. In his role as doctor and minister, Ian sees himself as a 'bridge person', an ordained theologian working in a hospital. He sees himself as a bridge between the Church and the world. Ian recognizes that for him to be effective and consistent with the Church's theology of ordained ministry, he needs to have one foot in the Church as well as having one foot in the world.

At times Ian has felt unsupported by the connexion. The circuit has also at times not understood his role, so it is a difficult place to be. For Ian, while the debate about ministers in sector appointment continues, he is sure that he is called to serve God in his workplace.

Conclusion

This chapter has looked at the ministry of those called to live out their ordination in the context of their working environment. It has explored the Anglican priest's calling to live out their ministry in the place of work and the Methodist presbyter's calling to live out their ministry in the secular environment of work. The chapter has investigated the historical and theological development of these ministries and set them in the context of ministry in the workplace.

Further reading

Hacking, R., 1990, *On the Boundary: A Vision for Non-Stipendiary Ministry*, Norwich: Canterbury Press.

Hodge, M., 1983, *Non-Stipendiary Ministry in the Church of England*, London: Church House Publishing.

Luscombe, P. and Shreeve, E. (eds), 2002, *What is a Minister?*, Peterborough: Epworth Press.

Pritchard, J., 2007, *The Life and Work of a Priest*, London: SPCK.

Torry, M. (ed.), 2006, *Diverse Gifts*, Norwich: Canterbury Press.

References

Advisory Board of Ministry, 1998, *Stranger in the Wings*, London: Church House Publishing.

Advisory Council for the Church's Ministry, 1968, *A Supporting Ministry*, London: Church House Publishing.

Advisory Council for the Church's Ministry, 1983, *Selection for Ministry: A Report on Criteria*, London: Church House Publishing.

Allen, R., 1923, *Voluntary Clergy*, London: SPCK.

Archbishops' Council, 1999, *Called to New Life: The World of Lay Disciples*, London: Church House Publishing.

Archbishops' Council, 2003, *Formation for Ministry within a Learning Church*, London: Church House Publishing.

Archbishops' Council, 2004, *Mission-Shaped Church: Church Planting and Fresh Expressions of Church in a Changing Context*, London: Church House Publishing.

Archbishops' Council, 2006, *Shaping the Future: New Patterns of Training for Lay and Ordained*, London: Church House Publishing.

Archbishops' Council Education Division, 2010, *Going for Growth: Transformation of Children, Young People and the Church*, London: Church House Publishing.

Astley, J., 2007, *Christ of the Everyday*, London: SPCK.

Avis, P., 2005, *A Ministry Shaped by Mission*, London: T. & T. Clark.

Bellamy, C., 2002, 'Calling or Cop-out? Sector Ministry Today', in P. Luscombe and E. Shreeve (eds), *What is a Minister?*, pp. 48–64, Peterborough: Epworth Press.

Boring, M. E., 1994, *The Gospel of Matthew* (The New Interpreters Bible), Nashville, TN: Abingdon Press.

Bowden, A., Francis, L. J., Jordan, E. and Simon, O., 2011, *Ordained Local Ministry in the Church of England*, London: Continuum.

British Council of Churches, 1976, *The Child in the Church*, London: British Council of Churches.

Brown, R., 2005, *Being a Deacon Today: Exploring a Distinctive Ministry in the Church and the World*, Norwich: Canterbury Press.

Carter, G., 2006, Presidential Address, www.methodistchurch.org.uk/index.cfm.

Chapman, I. A., 2004, 'The Call of a People', in C. Richardson (ed.), *This is Our Calling*, pp. 13–21, London: SPCK.

Cherry, S., 2011, *Barefoot Disciple*, London: Continuum.

Church of England, 1970, *Bishops' Regulations for the Selection and Training and Candidates for Auxiliary Ministry*, London: Church Assembly.

Church of England, 1987, *Regulations for Non-Stipendiary Ministry*, London: Church House Publishing.

Church of England, 1988, *Children in the Way*, London: Church House Publishing.

Church of England, 1991a, *Local NSM*, London: Church House Publishing.

Church of England, 1991b, *All God's Children*, London: Church House Publishing.

Church of England, 1998, *Selection for Reader Ministry Church of England* (ABM Policy Paper no. 7), London: Church House Publishing.

Church of England, 2001, *For Such a Time as This*, London: Church House Publishing.

Church of England, 2003, *Sharing the Good News with Children: The Church of England's Children's Strategy*, London: Church House Publishing.

Church of England, 2005a, *Children in the Midst*, London: Church House Publishing.

Church of England, 2005b, *Children Included: Guideline for Training Clergy, Readers, and Lay People in a Ministry among Children*, London: Church House Publishing.

Church of England, 2007a, *The Mission and Ministry of the Whole Church*, London: Church House Publishing.

Church of England, 2007b, *Common Worship: Ordination Services*, London: Church House Publishing.

Church of England, 2008, *Reader Upbeat: Quickening the Tempo of Reader Ministry in the Church Today*, General Synod Report GS1689. www.cofe.anglican.org/about/generalsynod/agendas/gs1689.rtf.

Church of England Board of Education, 1985, *All are Called: Towards a Theology of the Laity*, London: Church House Publishing.

Church of England Board of Education, 1987, *Called to be Adult Disciples*, London: Church House Publishing.

Coggan, D., 1998, *Meet Paul: An Encounter with the Apostle*, London: Triangle.

Consultative Group on Ministry among Children (CGMC), 2006, *Core Skills for Children's Work*, Oxford: Bible Reading Fellowship.

Costa, K., 2007, *God at Work: Living Every Day with Purpose*, London: Continuum.

Croft, S. and Walton, R., 2008, *Learning for Ministry: Making the Most of Study and Training*, London: Church House Publishing.

Dearing Report, 2001, *The Way Ahead: Church of England Schools in the New Millennium*, London: Church House Publishing.

DeLashmutt, M. W., 2008, *The Vicar's a Locksmith: The Rise of Lay-Clerics and the Decline of Christian Britain*, unpublished paper presented to the Society for the Scientific Study of Religion, Louisville, KY, USA.

Diocese of Salisbury, 2003, *The Distinctive Diaconate*, Salisbury: Sarum College Press.

Dunn, J., 1992, *Jesus' Call to Discipleship*, Cambridge: Cambridge University Press.

Edwards, P., 2004, 'The Call to Ministry', in C. Richardson (ed.), *This is Our Calling*, pp. 99–117, London: SPCK.

Fitzmyer, I. A., 1993, *According to Paul: Studies in the Theology of Paul*, New York: Paulist Press.

Francis, L. J. and Astley, J. (eds), 2002, *Children, Churches and Christian Learning*, London: SPCK.

Francis, L. J. and Atkins, P., 2000, *Exploring Luke's Gospel*, London: Mowbray.

Griffiths, P., 2006, 'Commissioned to Care: The Southwark Pastoral Auxiliary', in M. Torry (ed.), *Diverse Gifts: Varieties of Lay and Ordained Ministries in the Church Community*, pp. 65–77, Norwich: Canterbury Press.

Hacking, R., 1990, *On the Boundary: A Vision for Non-Stipendiary Ministry*, Norwich: Canterbury Press.

Hannaford, R., 1996, 'Foundations for an Ecclesiology of Ministry', in C. Hall and R. Hannaford (eds), *Order and Ministry*, pp 21–60, Leominster: Gracewing.

Heywood, D., 2011, *Reimagining Ministry*, London: SCM Press.

Higginson, R., 2002, *Questions of Business Life: Exploring Workplace Issues from a Christian Perspective*, London: Spring Harvest.

Hodge, M., 1983, *Non-Stipendiary Ministry in the Church of England*, London: Church House Publishing.

Hodge, M. and Mantle, J., 2001, 'Non-Stipendiary Ministry', in G. Kuhrt (ed.), *Ministry Issues for the Church of England*, pp. 221–2, London: Church House Publishing.

Jackson, S., 2008, 'The Methodist Diaconal Order: A Sign of the Diaconal Church', in D. Clark (ed.), *The Diaconal Church*, pp. 159–70, Peterborough: Epworth Press.

Kelly, R., 1999, *Exploring the Sacraments*, Buxhall: Kevin Mayhew.

Kinsella, B., 2011, *Tackling Knife Crime Together: A Review of Local Anti-Knife Crime Projects*, London: Home Office.

Mackenzie, A., 1997, *Faith and Work: A Thesis in Pastoral Theology*, Dunedin, New Zealand: University of Otago.

Methodist Church, 1968, *The Methodist Conference Agenda 1968*, London: Methodist Conference Office.

Methodist Church, 1999, *The Methodist Worship Book*, Peterborough: Methodist Publishing House.

Methodist Church, 2000, *Statements and Reports of the Methodist Church on Faith and Order, Volume Two 1984–2000, Part One*, Peterborough: Methodist Publishing House.

Methodist Church, 2002, *What is a Presbyter?*, London: Methodist Conference Office.

Methodist Church, 2004, *What is a Deacon?*, London: Methodist Conference Office.

Methodist Church, 2010, *Is God Calling You*, www.methodist.org.uk/candidates.

Methodist Church, 2012, *Steps in Candidating for Ordained Ministry in the Methodist Church*, www.methodist.org.uk/candidates.

Milburn, G. and Batty, M. (eds), 1995, *Workaday Preachers*, Peterborough: Methodist Publishing House.

Nappin, P., 2002, 'The Reader in the Parish', in G. W. Kuhrt and P. Nappin (eds), *Bridging the Gap: Reader Ministry Today*, pp. 11–18, London: Church House Publishing.

Oppenheimer, H., 1979, 'Ministry and Priesthood', in E. James (ed.), *Stewards of the Mysteries of God*, pp. 11–19, London: Darton, Longman & Todd.

Paul, L., 1964, *The Deployment and Payment of Clergy* (Paul Report), London: Church Information Office.

Pickard, S., 2009, *Theological Foundations for Collaborative Ministry*, Farnham: Ashgate.

Platten, S., 2010, 'The Grammar of Ministry and Mission', *Theology* 875, pp. 348–56.

Rowling, C. and Gooder, P., 2009, *Reader Ministry Explored*, London: SPCK.

Scott, S., 2006, 'Balancing Roles: The Non-Stipendiary Minister', in M. Torry (ed.), *Diverse Gifts*, pp. 51–64, Norwich: Canterbury Press.

Spina, F. A., 2001, 'Fourth Sunday in Lent Year A', in R. E. van Harn (ed.), *The Lectionary Commentary: Theological Exegesis for Sunday's Texts*, pp. 182–5, London: Continuum.

Stephenson, D., 2004, 'The Call of Disciples', in C. Richardson (ed.), *This is Our Calling*, pp. 55–66, London: SPCK.

Telford, J. (ed.), 1931, *The Letters of John Wesley*, London: Epworth Press.

Tiller, J., 1983, *A Strategy for the Church's Ministry* (Tiller Report), London: Church Information Office.

Wall, R. W., 2002, *The Acts of the Apostles* (The New Interpreters Bible), Nashville, TN: Abingdon Press.

World Council of Churches, 1982, *Baptism, Eucharist and Ministry* (Faith and Order Paper no. 111), Geneva: World Council of Churches.

Zabriskie, S. C., 1995, *Total Ministry: Reclaiming the Ministry of all God's People*, New York: Alban Institute.